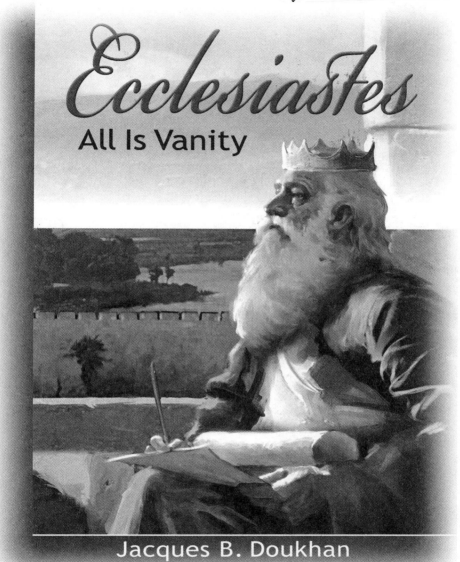

Ecclesiastes
All Is Vanity

Jacques B. Doukhan

Pacific Press® Publishing Association
Nampa, Idaho
Oshawa, Ontario, Canada
www.pacificpress.com

Inside design by Dennis Ferree
Cover design by Gerald Lee Monks
Cover illustration © Justinen Creative Group

ISBN 13: 978-0-8163-2177-3
ISBN 10: 0-8163-2177-9

Additional copies of this book are available by
calling toll free 1-800-765-6955
or by visiting <www.adventistbookcenter.com>.

06 07 08 09 10 · 5 4 3 2 1

Table of Contents

Table of Contents

Dedicated to the memory

of Elsbeth Uebersax-Nork,

my mother-in-law,

who passed away while I was writing this book.

She loved life and lived it to the fullest (Ecclesiastes 3:12).

CHAPTER 1

The Bragging Butterfly

According to legend, as Solomon was walking in his gardens and pondering the greatness of his works (he had just finished building the majestic temple), he overheard a busy conversation between two butterflies. Now, tradition says that Solomon was an expert in natural science and keen in the mysterious language of the animals; the biblical text records that Solomon "spoke also of animals, of birds, of creeping things, and of fish" (1 Kings 4:33). So it should be no wonder, then, that Solomon could understand the whispering of these two insects.

"With one blow of my wing," bragged Mr. Butterfly to his wife, "I could destroy this temple." Needless to say, Mrs. Butterfly was impressed. She admired her strong husband and his powerful muscles.

But Solomon did not like it and immediately summoned Mr. Butterfly to his office. "So," declared Solomon, "I understand that with the blow of one wing you can destroy my temple?"

"No! No!" stuttered the butterfly, trembling all over (this explains the habit of trembling that we see now among the butterflies). "I was just bragging to my wife; I just wanted her attention and her admiration."

Solomon smiled understandingly, then forgave the poor creature and let him go. As Mr. Butterfly came out of the palace, he met his trembling wife, who had been anxiously waiting to find out her husband's fate.

"What did Solomon tell you?" she asked.

Flexing his muscular wings once again, he looked his wife in the eye and said, "He begged me not to destroy his temple."

While this unusual story brings a smile to our faces, it takes us straight into the heart of Ecclesiastes. This is a book about the "vanity" of our work (for any of our work is vanity, even our most prestigious and most sacred work, like the wonderful temple of Solomon). Now *vanity* is a disturbing word, one that will threaten our security and prepare us for an uncomfortable yet essential truth that is found in the book of Ecclesiastes.

Let the reader be warned: Ecclesiastes is not always easy to follow. The thoughts are difficult and not always explicit. Also, the text belongs to another culture. It is written in Hebrew. We will need sometimes to refer to that language and, when necessary, provide a literal translation[1] in order that we may draw closer to the intention of the author. The author is a poet and a philosopher; he is a wise man. So we should expect him to pause on the beauty and the intricacies of a poem, and to make profound reflections on unusual ideas. The author is also a prophet and will venture into the troubling future. We recommend that the biblical text be read, along the way, chapter by chapter, slowly and repeatedly. The message of Ecclesiastes will not give itself to a speed reading. But if we pay close attention to his words, take *all* the words seriously, even those that seem contradictory and disturbing, and follow his sinuous path, we may well discover, beyond the hard sight of vanity, another face of God and another side of ourselves. And thus we may relearn to believe, to hope, and to live.

The Name: Ecclesiastes *(Qohelet)*

Ecclesiastes is a strange name for our twenty-first-century ears. But while it may mean nothing to us contemporary readers, the name is loaded with special meaning in the context of the Bible. The name *Ecclesiastes* is derived from the Greek word *ekklesia,* which means "the assembly" or "the church." It is the Greek translation of the Hebrew name *Qohelet,* which comes from the Hebrew word *qahal.*[2] An old Jewish commentary (*Qohelet Rabbah* 1:1) explains that *Qohelet* was so called because it refers to 1 Kings 8, where *qahal* means "the assembly" to whom Solomon was preaching (hence the common translation "Preacher" for *Qohelet*). Indeed the word *qahal* occurs seven times in that setting (1 Kings 8:1, 2, 14, 22, 55, 65).

It is also significant that the very name *Qohelet,* the Hebrew word for *Ecclesiastes,* is used seven times in the book of Ecclesiastes (1:1, 2, 12; 7:27; 12:8, 9, 10). Certainly this literary rhythm of seven, which marks the distribution of the name of the author in the book, is not accidental. We can see another example of this in *Song of Songs,* where the name of Solomon appears seven times (*Song of Songs* 1:1, 5; 3:7, 9, 11; 8:11, 12).[3]

It is clear that these connections between the biblical texts are intended to convey specific messages. First, they confirm Solomon as the author of the book; the connection with 1 Kings 8 associates *Qohelet*/Ecclesiastes with the Solomon of history, and the connection with the *Song of Songs* associates Ecclesiastes with the Solomon of literature. Although critical scholars have often challenged this authorship, the testimony of the book itself is in favor of the traditional attribution. The book contains many allusions to the time of Solomon and to Solomon himself—his asking God for wisdom, the building of the temple, his other building activities, his wealth, the cult of the temple, the end of his life, his old age, the political crisis of his succession, and so on. Many of these allusions will be indicated along the way in the book.

The reference to Solomon is affirmed already in the first verse; the author of the book is here explicitly identified as "the son of David, king in Jerusalem" (Ecclesiastes 1:1), an expression that clearly points to Solomon. In the Bible, the phrase *son of David* is used ten times, seven of which refer to Solomon. In 1:12 the phrase is even more specific: Ecclesiastes is designated as "king over Israel in Jerusalem," thus limiting the reference to Solomon, who was the only son of David to rule over Israel in Jerusalem. It is also noteworthy that in 1 Kings 8, the father-son relationship between David and Solomon is a recurring motif, appearing seven times (1 Kings 8:15, 17, 18, 19, 20, 24, 25, 26), with a hint at the building of the temple: "your son . . . shall build the house for My name" (1 Kings 8:19).

The antiquity of the book of Ecclesiastes has recently been suggested on the basis of a literary comparison with ancient Egyptian texts.[4] Indeed, Solomon, more than any other Jewish king, has been positively associated with Egypt. The introductory phrase, or superscription, of the book is characteristic of the ancient Egyptian didactic works of wisdom (the so-called instructions or *sebayt*): "The words of the Preacher, the son of David, king in Jerusalem . . . says the Preacher." It is noteworthy that the superscription of Ecclesiastes offers more literary affinities with the early instructions, from the Fifth Dynasty (2510–2460 B.C.) to the Twentieth Dynasty (1188–1069 B.C.), even though the reign of Solomon was contemporary to the Twenty-First Dynasty (1069–945 B.C.). Its closer affinity with the old Egyptian instructions, rather than with more recent ones, makes Solomon a reasonable option as the author of the book. It is important to realize this connection with ancient Egypt, for it not only helps us set the book in its appropriate time but also may shed light on some of its most intriguing reflections and expressions that are unique to this book within the Bible.

Indeed Solomon contracted political alliances with the Egyptian pharaohs; he asked for their assistance in his numerous construction works, imitated their customs, bought horses from them (1 Kings 10:28, 29), and followed their models of government and architecture.[5] He even married an Egyptian princess (1 Kings 11:1), an inconceivable compromise from an Egyptian point of view, since this made Solomon a potential heir to the throne of Egypt (royal succession was matrilineal in ancient Egypt). This unusual case reflects the Egyptian crisis of the time during the third intermediate period (1069–702 B.C.); the Pharaoh had lost his power and behaved as a weak king in need of support.

More importantly, in regard to the book of Ecclesiastes, Solomon's wisdom itself, his philosophical worldview, was associated with the Egyptian tradition. The Bible tells us that "Solomon's wisdom excelled . . . all the wisdom of Egypt" (1 Kings 4:30). This is not a negligible compliment when we know Egypt's reputation for its wisdom. The wise from "all nations, from all the kings of the earth" (1 Kings 4:34) recognized the superiority of his wisdom and came to hear it; he even received a visit from the Queen of Sheba (1 Kings 10:1–13), an Ethiopian province that was at that time under Egyptian influence. Solomon must have spoken Egyptian, and as a friend of Egypt and even a potential pharaoh, he must have been well versed in Egyptian literature.

It is no wonder that his book was so impregnated with Egyptian culture. The same style of debating with his inner self, in tension, is found in the Egyptian wisdom text *The Dispute Between a Man and His Ba.*[6] In another text, *The Complaints of Khakheperre-Sonb,*[7] one reads of conversations a man has with his heart. Also, in order to convey his message, Solomon used the Egyptian literary genre of the *sebayt:* a king coming to his old age writes to his son to instruct him and prepare him for the complex problems ahead of him. Likewise Solomon, author of Ecclesiastes, has grown old and wishes to share with his son the lessons he learned from his tumultuous life. To be sure, the book is full of allusions and references to the painful state of old age and the tragic issue of death.

Under the guidance of the Holy Spirit, this is the perspective of the book. An old king approaches his death and is haunted by his past; Solomon was born as the result of a crime (see 2 Samuel 12:1–25), and he often lived in tension between several cultures, but he is also frightened by the future, which does not belong to him anymore, and by the uncertainty that surrounds his succession. This particular perspective explains the disturbing tone of the book, the way it is written, and the trembling and the irony of its voice. Given the book's background, we can better understand its shocking and upsetting remarks and its repeated questions ("Who knows?" "Who can tell?" "Who can find out?" and "What profit has a man?").

Knowing the setting of the book even explains its many contradictions. At times Solomon sounds negative, skeptical, cynical, bitter, and pessimistic; he is mocking everything—possessions, honor, work, even wisdom and religion; he sees no sense to this life, which he finds unfair. But at other times, he calls for happiness and enjoyment of life; he encourages work and the search for wisdom; he praises righteousness; he sees meaning and justice in life and speaks of reward and punishment.

These contradictions are disturbing. The Talmud tells us that the ancient rabbis "wished to withdraw the book of Ecclesiastes because its words were self-contradictory" (*Shab.* 30b). The early church fathers allegorized the book in order to make it more acceptable to reason and orthodoxy. Modern critical scholars have suggested a literary solution: The book is a dialogue between two opposite views or simply a composite of several sources.

But contradiction and dissonance are precisely a part of Ecclesiastes' inspired message; if we try to eliminate the dissonance, we miss the point. What appears to be a contradiction is in fact a symptom of our human condition. Indeed, Ecclesiastes affirms the value of work, wisdom, life, and happiness, but all these good values—including religion and even righteousness—contain the potential of corruption and evil. Ecclesiastes shares here his lucid observations; without complacency or diplomacy he traces deception everywhere, even in the folds of virtue.

Everyone knows that evil is bad and clearly negative. The real problem is when evil hides itself in the good, when work becomes abusive and kills your soul and the soul of your neighbor, when wisdom becomes pride, when religion becomes hypocrisy and insensitivity to the "human" other, when righteousness becomes self-glorification and legalism. From a certain perspective, everything, not only the bad but also the good, is vanity. This is the Spirit-inspired perspective of the old king who grasped and verified it himself, painfully, in the flesh of his life. "All is vanity," yes, *all,* even the good.

The Motto: All Is Vanity *(hebel)*

Significantly, the word *vanity* (in Hebrew, *hebel*) is the first word of Qohelet's discourse and is also the key word of the book. It appears 38 times (out of the 73 occurrences in the whole Bible), in such strategic places of the discourse that some interpreters have been tempted to use it as a landmark to shape the structure of the book.[8] The word appears mostly in chapters 1 to 6, becoming more rare in chapters 7 to 12; this marks the two sections of the book. It is also noteworthy that the opening volley, " 'Vanity of vanities,' says the Preacher, 'Vanity of vanities, all is vanity,' " reappears verbatim in chapter 12. This indicates just how important the word *vanity* is to the book.

The word *hebel* is difficult to comprehend. On the basis of its primary meaning, "vapor" (Psalm 62:9; Isaiah 57:13), it is used in the Bible to designate what is not possible to grasp, what is passing, elusive, and without substance. *Hebel* expresses the ideas of negation, void, and nothingness (Psalm 78:33; Isaiah 30:7; 49:4; Job 9:25, etc.); the idea of shadow (Psalm 144:4) and of dream (Zechariah 10:2). It may also be applied to the ethical domain, to denounce lies and deception (Jeremiah 10:14), or to the religious domain, to denounce idols and false gods (Isaiah 57:13; Jeremiah 14:22, and other places). It is also the name of a person, Abel, the second son of Adam. In contrast to his older brother Cain, who occupies space and is a great achiever, Abel incarnates non-existence, the elusive vapor that will disappear without a trace.

Likewise in the book of Ecclesiastes, the meaning of *hebel* is not easy to define. Most interpreters have chosen to understand it in an abstract way, as a concept or a metaphor to suggest the ideas of emptiness and absurdity. The translation "vanity" has then been retained as the best option; it is vague enough to adapt itself to all the shades of the Hebrew word.

The discourse begins then with a strong accent on vanity. The emphasis is rendered not only by the repetition of the word in this verse,[9] but also by the superlative form "vanity of vanities." Finally and more importantly, it is emphasized in the phrase *"all* is vanity." This is a key phrase in Ecclesiastes, appearing seven times in the book.[10]

In fact, this message about vanity had already been sounded before the discourse began; the very first words that announced it, "words of *Qohelet*" (1:1), take us to the setting of 1 Kings 8, where Solomon was addressing the assembly *(qahal)* immediately after he had finished building the temple (1 Kings 7:51). First Kings 8:2 tells us that the event took place on the seventh month, Tishri (September/October), during the feast, that is, the Feast of Tabernacles, *Sukkot* (see Ezekiel 45:25; Nehemiah 8:14; John 7:37). *Sukkot* was the moment when the Israelites were supposed to remember their passage in the wilderness, when they lived under their tents; it was therefore a festive experience associated with the transitory character of life. Significantly, the book of Ecclesiastes is the biblical book that is to be read in the booths in order to accompany the liturgical flow of the Feast of Tabernacles. Biblical tradition has associated the dedication of the temple with *Sukkot,* the feast that reminds us of the vanity of our lives, and also with the book of Ecclesiastes, which preaches about that vanity. Ironically, Solomon chose this particular setting of *Sukkot* to dedicate his temple.

Yes even the temple, Solomon's greatest, holiest achievement, was associated with vanity! The expression "the words of *Qohelet*" points back to the dedication of the temple. Solomon goes back to the be-ginnings and remembers; it is as if he retraced his journey and real-ized the path he had taken. This little allusion places the book of Ecclesiastes in the heart of Solomon's repentance, while lucidly, painfully, he measures the vanity of his achievements, even the tem-ple. Mr. Butterfly's bragging about the temple is not only timely; it fits the moment of Solomon's spiritual and emotional journey.

The Scope: The World

Yet the words of Ecclesiastes transcend the historical person of Solomon. The horizon is the world. A number of evidences suggest the universal scope of the book. First, Ecclesiastes makes a great number of allusions to the book of Genesis: the Creation story, the Fall, the curse, sin, evil, death, Abel, (whose name means "vanity"), and Cain (whose name means "achievement"), the reference to the angel of God. Ecclesiastes is probably the biblical book that refers or alludes most to Genesis. Second, the book is brimming with univer-sal language: expressions such as "under the sun," "under heaven," "on the earth," "man" (called Adam), and the use of the generic name *Elohim* for God rather than the particular Israelite name *YHWH*. The book's topics are universal: death, old age, youth, life, love, women, evil, suffering, injustice, God, happiness, work, and ethics. The book deals with many aspects of religious life, such as faith, doubt, prayer, commitments, offerings, and the command-ments of God. It addresses a number of sensitive and complex theo-logical issues such as Creation, judgment, righteousness by works, grace, sin, hope, inspiration and revelation, the state of the dead, prophecy, and apocalypse. The book speaks even to secular, nonreli-gious people, using philosophical language, and appealing to logic and existential reflections. References to God are rare, or implicit, as are references to the cult and the temple life. In fact, Ecclesiastes refers more to humanity than he refers to God. The book sounds more like a philosophical exploration of the human condition than a theological tome. Its environment is the marketplace: work, sleep-ing, eating and drinking, political life, the city, sports, and enter-tainment.

Perhaps this is the book of the Bible that resonates the most in our postmodern times. After the Holocaust and September 11, we realize that optimism, traditional values, and coherent systems of thought do not fit anymore. We now face a world that is more and more beyond human control, a world in which—left only to itself and not going beyond itself—indeed "all is vanity."

---

1. We will use the New King James Version (NKJV), unless indicated otherwise.

2. As for its morphology in *Qohelet,* it indicates a professional function; see for instance Nehemiah 7:57, where the same form is used to designate the function of a scribe (see P. Joüon-Muraoka, *A Grammar of Biblical Hebrew* [Rome: Pontificio Istituto Biblico, 1991], §89 b).

3. It is interesting to note that in both books the use of the names follows the same strategic distribution (beginning, middle, end).

4. See Jacques Doukhan, *"Sous le Soleil", Une lecture de Qohelet à la lumière de l'Egypte ancienne (Le prologue, 1:1-11)* ["Under the Sun," A Reading of Qohelet in the Light of Ancient Egypt (The Prologue, 1:1–11)], M. A. thesis in Egyptology, University of Montpellier, France, 2004, 12.

5. See J. D. Currid, *Ancient Egypt and the Old Testament* (Grand Rapids, Mich.: Baker Books, 1997), 165-171.

6. See M. Lichtheim, *Ancient Egyptian Literature* (Berkeley: University of California Press, 1973), vol. 1, 163–169. The text belongs to the Twelfth Dynasty (1990–1785 B.C.).

7. Ibid., 145–149. This work belongs to the Eighteenth Dynasty (1550–1305 B.C.).

8. See A. Wright, "The Riddle of the Sphinx: The Structure of the Book of Qoheleth," *Catholic Biblical Quarterly* 30 (1968), 313–334; compare D. Miller, *Symbol and Rhetoric in Ecclesiastes, the Place of* Hebel *in Qohelet's Work* (Atlanta: Society of Biblical Literature, 2002), 23.

9. The ancient rabbis counted the word seven times: Vanity (1) of vanities (2), vanity (1) of vanities (2), all is vanity (1)." See T. A. Perry, *Dialogues with Kohelet: The Book of Ecclesiastes, Translation and Commentary* (University Park, Pa.: The Pennsylvania State University Press, 1993), 24.

10. 1:2, 14; 2:11, 17; 3:19; 11:8; 12:8.

11. Humanity is mentioned forty-eight times as opposed to forty times for God.

CHAPTER 2

Ground Zero

Ecclesiastes, like the Bible itself, begins with the beginning: the Creation of the world. After seven repetitions of the Hebrew word *hebel,* "vapor-vanity," as the "motto" of the book (Ecclesiastes 1:2), the author asks a rhetorical question, "What profit . . . under the sun?" (1:3), placing us in a cosmic perspective ("under the sun"). Ecclesiastes (the name we will give to the author) is intrigued by the back and forth movements of all the basic cosmic elements of Creation: the sun, the earth, the wind, the waters, and humans are described in full activity. And yet nothing really new happens: no advantage is gained. It all seems so purposeless. This beautiful poem about the universe will set the tone to his reflection throughout the book.

The skill of the poet and his philosophical intention transpire in the style and in the construction of the poem. There is repetition of the words "generation . . . generation" (1:4), "the sun . . . the sun" (1:5), "the wind . . . the wind" (1:6), "the rivers . . . the rivers" (1:7), "the sea . . . the sea" (1:7). Many action verbs are also repeated: "to go," "to turn around," and "to rise." These repetitions give an impression of both monotony and business.[1] The point of the poem is that everything repeats, always returning to the beginning.

It is also remarkable that all these movements are not happening at random; they reflect the successive steps of the Genesis Creation story (Genesis 1:1–2:4), as if history had to come back to its starting

16

point and be redone. Notice the many parallels between Ecclesiastes 1 and Genesis 1 and 2:

- 1:2, "all is vanity"/state of pre-Creation (Genesis 1:1, 2).
- 1:3, "under the sun"/light and sky (first and second days, Genesis 1:3–8).
- 1:4, the earth/the earth "under the sky" (third day, Genesis 1:9–13).
- 1:5, 6, sunrise and sunset; wind of the North and of the South/ day-night and seasons (fourth day, Genesis 1:14–19).
- 1:7, rivers and sea in movement/life in water (fifth day, Genesis 1:20–23).
- 1:8, humans who speak, see, and hear/creation of humans (sixth day, Genesis 1:24–31).
- 1:9, humans who do not remember ("nothing new")/end of Creation (Sabbath, Genesis 2:1–3).

From this parable about the endless movements of the elements of Creation, from step to step, Ecclesiastes draws a consistent message: all movements consistently return to their origin and therefore never move beyond ground zero. "All is vanity" (1:2), the motto set forth in verse 2, is thus confirmed. "All" *(kol)* is a key word of the Creation story (Genesis 1:30, 31; 2:1, 2, 3, 5); it embraces the whole world of Creation. The same cosmic perspective strikes again in the question that introduces the movements of the elements of the world: "What profit has a man from all his labor / In which he toils under the sun"? (1:3) The word *all* is used here in connection with Adam, and the whole is placed "under the sun."

Vanity Under the Sun

The reference to the sun is special in the book of Ecclesiastes. Of the 131 references to the sun in the whole Bible, 35 of them occur in Ecclesiastes, and 29 of these are found in the key phrase *under the sun*. This is the most recurring phrase in the book of Ecclesiastes— the only book in which this expression appears.

On the other hand, the expression *under the sun* is an idiomatic expression in ancient Egyptian, in which it is even commonly represented through the hieroglyphic sign of the sun placed above the preposition *under*. This expression, which evokes the cycle of the sun, not only places us in a cosmic perspective but also points to the continuous repetition of that cycle. Significantly, the Egyptian phrase means "regularly" or "daily." Our situation under the sun relegates us to an endless repetition and never to any new production.

"Under the sun," then, the author sees only "vanity." It is interesting to notice the place of *hebel*, "vanity," in parallel to the Creation story; it appears just before creation starts, at the moment that corresponds to the stage of pre-Creation (1:2). This stage is described in the Genesis Creation story as "without form, and void *[tohu wabohu]*; and darkness . . ." (Genesis 1:2). The same meaning of *hebel* is confirmed in the Bible, where the word *hebel* is associated with the expressions "without form" *(tohu)* and "darkness" *(hoshek)*. In the book of Isaiah, the word *tohu*, "nothing," is related to the word *hebel*, "vanity": "I have spent my strength for nothing *[tohu]* and in vain *[hebel]*" (Isaiah 49:4); likewise, in the book of Ecclesiastes, the stillborn child "comes in vanity *[hebel]* and departs in darkness *[hoshek]*" (6:4).

If we interpret the word *hebel* in that connection, it means more than just "vanity"; it refers to the stage that preceded Creation. We did not move beyond *tohu wabohu*; it is as if the event of Creation did not take place. All the cosmic movements were in vain. This observation will be tested in the laboratory of the cosmos: the generations, the sun and the wind, the rivers, and the words.

The Passing of Generations

As soon as one generation comes it goes. This cyclic idea of come and go is already contained in the Hebrew word *dor*, "generation," whose primary meaning is "circle."[2] And the cycle of generations is continually renewed. The process is eternal; it will always be like this. Through the word *generation*, the Hebrew expresses this idea of eternity ("from generation to generation," Exodus 17:16). But for Ecclesiastes, the generations are not eternal; instead, the movement of "come and go" makes the generations continually passing.

The words that describe this movement belong to the language of death. The word *go* is often used to refer to death (1:4; 3:20; 5:15, etc.), and when it is associated with the word *come*, as here, it always means "death" (5:15, 16; 6:4; 11:9, 10). For Ecclesiastes, the passing of generations is an expression of death.

The only thing left, says Ecclesiastes, is the earth, which alone "abides forever" (1:4). The only durable eternity is the earth. But this is not an eternity of life, the eternal prolongation of the present life, as the ancient Egyptians believed. Rather, it is an eternity attached to an earth void of life and history; it is an eternity of death; an eternity of non-eternity.

The Sun and the Winds

The sun goes to the extremities of the world, yet it always comes back to its starting point, "the place where it arose" (1:5), that is, the east. This cycle of the sun again betrays the intention of Ecclesiastes, who insists that everything ends where it started. He says that the sun starts in the east and also ends in the east, while we would have expected it to end in the west,[3] as is the case in Egyptian tradition. The sun is compared to a racer pressing toward the finish line, panting and striving toward the goal, "the place." The Hebrew word translated "place," *maqom*, is generally used in a cosmic context[4] and may refer to the Promised Land (Genesis 13:14–17) or to the birthplace (Ezekiel 21:35). The sun languishes to the east, its birthplace, its promised land. The whole accent is put on this place of arrival. Frustratingly, though, we are still at the same point, at the stage of sunrise; nothing has been accomplished. Ironically, contrary to the Egyptian tradition that associates sunrise with the ideas of life and hope, here sunrise takes us again to ground zero, conveying the idea of hopelessness, forever stuck at the point of *hebel,* the "not yet" of Creation.

As the sun generates the passing of days, in response the wind brings the passing of seasons. In verse 6, in the Hebrew sentences, there is no subject for the verbs *to go* and *to turn around.* While the verse places the movements of the wind toward the south, this seems to be an immediate extension of the movements of the sun (in verse 5). This phrasing leaves the real meaning of the passage ambiguous: either the sun or the wind may be considered the subject of the verbs in verse 6. This relation between the sun and the wind is also confirmed by the abnormal fact that only the directions south and north are mentioned for the wind; which suggests a certain complementary connection between the two movements of the wind, south and north, and those of the sun, east and west.

Moreover, the parallel between the south and north movement of the wind and the east and west movement of the sun suggests a correspondence of a climatic nature. The east, which brings the heat and the light of the sun, corresponds to the south, a place associated with heat and luminosity (Job 37:17). The west, which brings the cold of the night, corresponds to the north, which is the place of cold and darkness and is associated with clouds and rain (Proverbs 25:23). Like the passing of days, the seasons turn and finally come back *(shub)* to their starting point. Indeed the four back and forth phases of the wind suggest that its departure point is the north and its final destination is again the north. It

1. "goes toward the south": direction south (from the north)
2. "turns around to the north": direction north (from the south)
3. "whirls about": direction south (from the north)
4. "comes again on its circuit": direction north (from the south)

All this agitation, then, is for nothing. All these returns of seasons do not take us forward, because we end up still at the beginning, the north where the wind came from originally. Now, in biblical tradition the wind of the north is associated with destruction[5] (Jeremiah 1:14; 46:20). We have not yet gone beyond ground zero, the stage of chaos that characterizes destruction. Significantly, the wind of the north, the wind of destruction, is identified with *hebel.*

The Rivers and the Words

In spite of the pouring of the rivers, the sea is never full (1:7). This idea is typical of the ancient Middle East worldview, which imagined the earth surrounded by the great primordial ocean ("the sea") to which all the rivers were flowing.[6]

This is the same lesson taught by the other cosmic elements: In spite of all the busy agitations, we have not progressed; at the end of all our pains, we are still at the starting point, at the uncreated stage. But this latest imagery brings a more tragic note. First, we understand that this destiny is unavoidable, for the waters of the rivers are by nature identified with the primeval chaos; therefore, they will not produce anything new. Not only do they originate in the primordial waters; they *are* primordial waters. But second, and what is more serious, is that at this return of the rivers lies hopelessness. For, with certainty, all the rivers return to the sea. History has failed completely. The landscape of the end is the same as at the beginning, when the earth was still only a watery mass, void from the word of the Creator (Genesis 1:2), *hebel.*

Finally, humans are in the same predicament (1:8–11). The repetition of words and the parallelism of syntax between verse 7 ("all the rivers run . . . not full") and verse 8 (all the words[7] . . . not full) indicate a connection between the continuous flow of the rivers and human activity. Like the rivers always flowing to the sea, these words, expressions of human wisdom, are "exhausting" (*NIV:* "wearisome"). They have no end and are poured ad infinitum . . . countless words and concepts. Like the rivers, which never fill the sea, these words never "satisfy," and the ears, like the sea, are never filled. Like those rivers, which disappear forever in the abyss, the words do not contribute anything to the debate; finally, "they do not express," that is—they do not say anything.

Associated with the water element and, thus, identified with the stage of pre-Creation, the human word means nothingness. Unlike the ancient Egyptian scribes, for whom the word had power of eternity and control over history, Ecclesiastes deplores its inefficiency. The word does not add anything. The word does not say anything. Thus the word does not leave any trace, does not go beyond the stage of the mere breath-vapor of *hebel.*

In the beginning, Ecclesiastes had asked the question "What profit has a man from all his labor / In which he toils under the sun?" (1:3). In that question, Ecclesiastes was wondering about whether this human work could contribute something, whether it brought anything new. The answer is negative: "There is nothing new under the sun" (verse 9). Ecclesiastes' response embraces the whole of the universe. The word "all" *(kol),* which qualifies the word "new," reminds us of the other occurrences of "all" *(kol),* which precede it and embrace them all, because it is the last one (verses 2, 3, 7, 8). Nothing can be new, even the word of wisdom, adds Ecclesiastes in verse 10. And if anyone would boast to say something new, it is simply because he forgot that this word has already been said, because there is no memory from one generation to the next (verse 11). And if the word of the wise has already been said, this means that even the word of the wise did not go beyond the beginning. Even wisdom is *hebel.*

21

Ecclesiastes does not spare anything—from the tireless movements of the universe, to the profound words of wisdom, everything is "vanity." It is as if nothing happened since the beginning of time, more precisely, since even before Creation itself. It is as if we were still "without form and void" (Genesis 1:2). The movements of the world confirm that lesson: "That which has been is what will be" (Ecclesiastes 1:9). Ecclesiastes is not here taking an Egyptian or Greek sort of cyclic view of history. What he observes is not cyclic, but static. "There is nothing new under the sun" (1:9). This emphatic rejection of the new is foreign to biblical thought; biblical thought prefers to affirm the new (Psalm 96:1; Jeremiah 31:31; Isaiah 43:19). On the other hand, this rejection of the new is a very common idea in Egyptian tradition. Yet, while in Egyptian tradition this idea is positive, expressing the idea of eternity, in Ecclesiastes it becomes negative. The author's point is that history is not moving; nothing new happens, and, therefore, all is vanity.

Ecclesiastes' reflection is not merely a contemplative poem about nature, the sunset, and the flow of the sea, or a mere existential reflection about the absurdity of life. Rather, Ecclesiastes' perspective is cosmic. This is why he starts his argument with Creation and the universe, telling us that the world is a failure, a tragic abortion. He tells us that we all are the "vapor" of the precreation; "all is vanity," including us. From this cosmic ground zero, the *tohu wabohu,* "without form and void," Ecclesiastes invites us to think.

While the prologue (1:2–11) is written in the third person, at verse 12 the text shifts to the first person. Ecclesiastes leaves behind the tone of the parable and the object lessons of the movements of Creation and comes back to himself to think about wisdom. "I set my heart to seek and search out by wisdom" (1:13), and "I set my heart to know wisdom" (1:17).

The Search for Wisdom

For Ecclesiastes, the state of the world is so tragic that the use of wisdom will not help: "What is crooked cannot be made straight, / And what is lacking cannot be numbered" (1:15). The world is hopeless; wisdom is useless. Any human attempt to repair the world is ridiculous; it leads nowhere. Ecclesiastes is adamant: "I have seen all the works that are done under the sun; and indeed, all is vanity and grasping for the wind" (1:14).

Does that mean that all the New Year's resolutions and efforts we invest to improve our character are vanity? Does that mean that all the noble moves of the heart and of the hand to relieve pain, war, hunger, and oppression are vanity? Does this mean that all the great revolutions that change the course of history are not accomplishing anything and are, too, vanity? Does that mean that all the missionary activities to share the good news of God and save the world are vanity?

Certainly this interpretation is morally and spiritually unacceptable, for it promotes irresponsibility. Yet such a mindset may seduce some who are either naturally indifferent to the misery of the world or simply too occupied with dreams of another world.

This, however, is not what Ecclesiastes is saying. The text does not suggest that we should refrain from doing something about this world. Ecclesiastes' point is not about the value of the work itself but rather about the value of human wisdom in that enterprise; it concerns the illusion that our wisdom could help solve the problem.

Ecclesiastes argues that, as far as the fate of the world is concerned, this wisdom is useless; it is as if it would oppose the work of God. And indeed, the same question, "who can make straight what He has made crooked?" reappears in 7:15, where it explicitly applies to "the work of God." God is implied as the agent of the brokenness of the world, pointing to the curse that God inflicted on the earth following the fall (Genesis 3:17, 18). Therefore, no human wisdom can help reverse the tragic condition of the world; this condition is determined by God Himself. It is "the work of God." What Ecclesiastes has in mind here is not so much our responsibility toward evil in the world, but rather the foolish idea that our human work or wisdom may be able to affect its crooked nature. In regard to the God-determined fate of the earth, wisdom is vanity.

This view is immediately confirmed in the next verse, where Ecclesiastes refers again to his own wisdom, which he qualifies as superior over "all who were before me" (1:16). It's as though he is proclaiming, "If I, Ecclesiastes, being wiser than any other before me, have not been able to solve the problem, don't think that your wisdom will be more successful." Here the Preacher inserts a subtle irony. He has just warned us in verse 10 that no one should claim to be wiser than those who came before. Now, pretending to fall into that trap himself, he anticipates the presumption of the one who would make such a claim, hoping to neutralize such a claim to human wisdom. No wisdom, no matter how great, will provide us with the solution.

On the contrary, argues Ecclesiastes, the search of wisdom will produce more problems: "For in much wisdom is much grief, / And he who increases knowledge increases sorrow" (1:18). Not only will wisdom not solve the problem, and is therefore vanity; it also will produce more problems. The search for wisdom is therefore vanity. Does that mean that the search for wisdom, the intellectual quest to understand, is to be dismissed? Is this an impetus to laziness and anti-intellectualism? No—this is not what Ecclesiastes has in mind. He does not discourage intellectual effort. He could not! He just observed that this work is, in fact, sacred. Although the intellectual effort is essentially human, it is qualified as a religious duty imposed by God upon humans: "This grievous task God has given to the sons of man, by which they may be exercised" (1:13).

For Ecclesiastes, this warning against wisdom is not the search for wisdom per se, but the unexpected product of wisdom, which is "grief" and "sorrow." Lucidity, the capacity to see reality as it is, does not make us happier. On the contrary, it brings anger, revolt, and pain; it makes us more critical or more bitter; certainly it makes us less submissive, or more afraid and anguished. Suppose we learn that we are facing a life-threatening disease or discover that our spouse is unfaithful? As our wisdom increases (by learning this disturbing truth), it automatically is accompanied by worries and suffering.

Thus, is it sometimes preferable not to know? This would be cowardice and self-deception. As human beings, we choose the pain of knowledge over the happiness of ignorance. This choice reflects our human nature. The philosopher Pascal noted that this knowledge is what makes us who we are, superior over nature and the animal. "Man knows that he will die; the animal does not." Indeed, it is better to be an unhappy man who knows than to be a satisfied imbecile.

The words of Ecclesiastes contain another truth that strikes in the heart of civilization; more than ever our lives witness every day the cruel and ironic pertinence of this observation. We thought that modernity and progress, the fruit of wisdom and knowledge, would solve our problems and simplify our lives. Yet we have experienced that the more we "increased knowledge," the more we "increased sorrow" (1:18), the more problems we created, and the further we complicated our lives.

At the turn of the twentieth century, science was full of promise; we believed that it would bring an end to many problems. Indeed some of our troubles disappeared, but a whole cortege of others came along to make us regret the passing of the good old days, when work was easier, communications more human, and life in general much less stressful. True, this nostalgic song deploring the ravages of progress has always been sung—Ecclesiastes' words testify to that. Since that time, nothing has changed. We keep progressing and regretting, as if we have forgotten, or still believe, that we will do better. But history has shown that as far as progress and the increase of knowledge are concerned, ambivalence is an unavoidable part of the package. Therefore, we had better optimistically accept living with progress, hoping to "wisely" maintain the delicate balance between the two opposite forces.

An old, satiric cartoon portrays a man walking along, looking up at an airplane flying. He wonders how safe it is to have those planes in the air. But as he continues to walk, while looking up at the airplane, he falls into a hole and dies. We should then not worry too much about the planes; until, of course, the negative side of progress prevails and progress is stopped, suddenly, brutally, by the arms of progress. Today, more than ever, in an age of weapons of mass destruction, this kind of worry could take on cosmic proportions. It seems that, in addition to all the mishaps of progress that are not excluded from Ecclesiastes' denunciation, a tragic and cosmic prospect lies on the horizon of his warning: the return to ground zero. Ecclesiastes calls this vanity. When ethics are no longer in control, when wisdom is being served by humans rather than humans being served by wisdom, when wisdom becomes the end and no longer the means—then the sacredness of human life and dignity are sacrificed on the altar of wisdom. Ecclesiastes is concerned with this ultimate outcome of wisdom, the deceptive idea that wisdom is the final solution. The ultimate temptation of wisdom is wisdom itself, that is, to take the assignment of the search for wisdom God has put upon us, and transform it into a way to take God's place.

This was the temptation of Eve in the Garden of Eden: "God knows," the serpent had argued, "that if you take that fruit of the tree of knowledge, your eyes will be opened, and you will be like God, knowing good and evil" (see Genesis 3:5). Eve was seduced by the argument: "When the woman saw that the tree was . . . desirable to make one wise, she took of its fruit and ate" (Genesis 3:6). And we know the rest of the story.

It is Ecclesiastes' story, and ours as well.

---

1. See C. L. Seow, *Ecclesiastes: A New Translation with Introduction and Commentary*, The Anchor Bible (New York: Doubleday, 1997), 111, 112.

2. This meaning is attested in Arabic where the word *daur*, etymologically related to our Hebrew word *dor*, means "phase," "a period of time," but also "rotation," "revolution," or "cycle"; see Johannes G. Botterweck, "dôr," in *Theological Dictionary of the Old Testament*, ed. Johannes G. Botterweck and Helmer Ringgren (Grand Rapids, Mich.: Eerdmans, 1974), 172.

3. In Egyptian tradition, the west, the place of sunset, is interpreted as arrival; see Jan Assmann, *Egyptian Solar Religion in the New Kingdom: Re, Amun and the Crisis of Polytheism*, Studies in Egyptology (London: Kegan Paul International, 1995), 63.

4. See J. Gamberoni, *"maqôm,"* in *Theological Dictionary of the Old Testament*, ed. Johannes G. Botterweck and Helmer Ringgren (Grand Rapids, Mich.: Eerdmans, 1974), 536.

5. It is interesting that in Egyptian tradition the wind of the north is associated with the beginning of life. The refreshing wind originating from the north is the symbol of the primary breath of life. In the Egyptian *Book of the Dead* (ch. 183, 1. 5–7), Osiris, the god of death, recovers life when he receives the breath of the wind of the north. It is possible that Ecclesiastes also has this tradition in mind; in that case, one may wonder whether this identification of the wind of the north with the "not yet" of Creation is not intentional, a subtle and ironic allusion to the vapor *hebel*.

6. See Christian D. Ginsburg, *The Song of Songs and Coheleth (Commonly Called the Book of Ecclesiastes)*, The Library of Biblical Studies (New York: Ktav Publishing House, 1970), 363.

7. The Hebrew word *debarim* means both "things" and "words"; we have adopted the translation "words" on the basis of its association with "man who cannot express it," which implies the mouth, and in connection to the eye and the ear (see also verse 1).

CHAPTER 3

Joy, Work, Wisdom, and God

Our life will now be "tested." Ecclesiastes uses that specific term: "Come now, I will *test* you" (Ecclesiastes 2:1). And the test concerns three values of life—joy, work, and wisdom. We must test what makes our human life bearable, useful, and meaningful in order to see if there is something "good" in them. This is the purpose of the test: "Till I might see what is good for the sons of men to do under heaven all the days of their lives" (2:3). Considering the importance of Creation in the book of Ecclesiastes, let's see how the word "good" *(tov)* was used in the Genesis creation account in order to see how we might understand it in Ecclesiastes.

In Genesis *good* is also associated with the word *to see,* namely, in the phrase that recurs seven times as a refrain: "God saw that it was good" (Genesis 1:4, 10, 12, 18, 21, 25, 31). Ecclesiastes' test will check whether there is something left from the "good" work of creation. The results are negative. He invariably comes to the same conclusion— "vanity"—also repeated seven times, like the refrain of the Creation story (2:1, 11, 15, 19, 21, 23, 26). Seven times we are reminded of *hebel,* the state that describes precreation. *Hebel,* the nothingness of pre-Creation, is what characterizes the human experience.

Joy Is Vanity

All the facets of happiness are included in this test: gladness, pleasure, and rejoicing (2:1); laughter (2:2); and even the feasting of the senses under the effect of wine (2:3).

Ecclesiastes specifies that he is the one who conducts the test: "*I* will test you with mirth" (2:1), "*I* said of laughter" (2:2), "*I* searched . . . while guiding my heart with wisdom" (2:3). From his own observation and with the help of his wisdom, Ecclesiastes reaches the conclusion that pleasure is vanity (2:1), laughter is madness (2:2), mirth does not accomplish anything (2:2), and wine is folly (2:3). No reasoning, argument, or evidence are provided. The only guarantee that Ecclesiastes is right is that he always maintained that his wisdom was with him. He never lost control. He remained lucid in the midst of his joy, even when joy was ecstatic and irrational.

It is, then, from within himself, subjectively, that he draws the lesson that joy is vanity. For the joy Ecclesiastes refers to is not the product of an external factor; it is Ecclesiastes himself who is the author of his joy. He gives himself all kinds of pleasure. As king, he could afford it: "Whatever my eyes desired I did not keep from them, / I did not withhold my heart from any pleasure" (2:10).

We don't need to be kings today to resonate with Solomon. In our democratic society and in our pleasure-centered civilization, "all kinds of pleasures" are available. Solomon does not evaluate the quality or ethics of those joys. All kinds of joys are included here, innocent or dangerous, lawful or lawless, plain or sophisticated—the reasonable joy of a good meal or of a comfortable evening in front of our TV set; the exciting joy of the dangerous sport; the honorable joy of reading an edifying book; the spiritual joy of singing a hymn; the esthetic joy of listening to great music or contemplating a piece of art; the sensual joy of sex, of smelling a flower, or of swimming in the sea. And we do not want to mention here the other joys—the sinful ones, the unethical ones, the criminal joys.

All the joys are under his judgment; they are all vanity. This may sound strange and shocking, but the reason for this unqualified judgment is simple. Ecclesiastes is not concerned with the moral or spiritual value of joy, but with its reality. Indeed, joy is in essence an inner experience, a state of the mind. For Ecclesiastes the experience of joy takes place in the heart: "for my heart rejoiced" (2:10). Whether it is an emotion or a sensation, a mental, sentimental, or physical experience, it remains something within us; it has no reality, no substance in itself. Joy is of the same nature as a dream or mirage. It could be an illusion, the product of imagination or self-deception. This is why Ecclesiastes could evaluate it from within himself and perceive from there that it is vanity.

Joy is also vanity because of the time element; it doesn't last. His evaluations of joy belong to the present and are given while the experience is lived. Because his wisdom and lucidity keep him awake and fully aware of the instant, the essence of joy is its present dimension. It is an enjoyment of the moment. Indeed the experience of joy is short. Very soon we are back to the sad and ordinary reality of life. And the void that comes after joy is all the more painful, because the experience of joy was so intense.

We understand, then, why many people use artificial means to prolong their joy. Some drink. Just as Ecclesiastes refers to the joy associated with wine, many today claim joy as the good reason behind their drinking. Of course, we could add the other artificial drugs that give a quick "high." We know that these joys are false, full of deception and death. These artificial joys epitomize vanity at its best.

Even laughter is under Ecclesiastes' scrutiny. It is diagnosed as "madness." There is something irrational about laughter. When the clown stumbles or when we laugh at a joke, it is the absurdity of the situation that makes us laugh. Ecclesiastes is right. Laughter does not accomplish anything. It is not productive, not useful—and does not last. Even if we have a good time, laughter remains a simple vanity. It is also deceitful; there is often profound sadness behind the mask of the clown or our bursts of laughter. According to Ecclesiastes, all these joys, initiated and shaped by our own hands, do not deserve our respect or attention, for they do not have value or even reality in themselves.

Work Is Vanity

The vanity of work does not lie in work itself. It is the fear that all the work, all the accumulation of wealth, of experience, and so on, will benefit someone else. For Ecclesiastes it is the prospect of his succession. The text mentions this apprehension in four verses (2:12, 18, 21, 26) and gives the explicit reason in verse 18: "I must leave it to the man who will come after me."

The text alludes to Solomon and looks like a resume of the king's achievements: the grandeur of his works (2:4, 9; compare 1 Kings 10:23), his fabulous wealth (2:7, 8; compare 1 Kings 3–11), his silver and gold[1] (2:8; compare 1 Kings 10:14–29), his acquisition of cattle (2:7; compare 1 Kings 8:5), and his many women (2:8; compare 1 Kings 11:1). This allows us to think that the four verses from Ecclesiastes mentioned before (2:12, 18, 21, 26) are also reflecting Solomon's problem of succession and his own anguish in regard to the political turmoil surrounding his succession (1 Kings 12).

Yet, beside the autobiographical note, we can perceive a universal truth. All our accumulation, whether of money or properties, will not accompany us to the tomb. The parable of Jesus reminds us of the vanity of the fool who lays up treasure for himself (Matthew 12:21). He dies, and all this accumulation is for nothing.

Ecclesiastes adds another fear: this treasure carefully amassed will one day pass to another's hands, perhaps even to hostile ones. Not only will his work be enjoyed by someone else (2:26) who may not make any better use of the inheritance than he did (2:12), but there is also the chance that all our work may be disfigured or even destroyed (2:19). For all these reasons, amassing wealth is the equivalent of doing nothing. It is pure vanity.

The confession about the vanity of his own work is also dramatic because Solomon was a hard worker, someone who had achieved many things. The Bible remembers him as a great builder (1 Kings 7:1–12; 9:15–28) and our text lists a great number of his works. From verse 4 to verse 11, the word "make" ('asah), appears seven times to describe his achievements (2:4, 5, 6, 8, 11), which Ecclesiastes qualifies as vanity (2:11).

It is interesting that the word *to make* is also an important key word in the Creation story (Genesis 1:11, 12, 16, 25, 26, 31 and 2:2, 3, 4). The fundamental difference, however, lies in the fact that in the Creation story, the subject of the verb *to make* is God. In Ecclesiastes the text suggests, by means of the phrase "I built" (banah) (verse 4), that Solomon had replaced God in the task of "making." This phrase happens to be a key expression in the biblical text that reports on the building of the temple. In 1 Kings 8, from verse 13 to verse 20, the phrase "to build" is used seven times referring to God: "I built for you." In Ecclesiastes, however, the phrase refers to Solomon himself: "I built for myself." Our text seems, then, to indicate that even the building of the temple was implied in the list of vanities, an irony that is worth noticing (remember the bragging butterfly). When Ecclesiastes says that all his works are vanity, he is saying that even holy works may qualify as such, because they are often self-centered. Our "building of the temple," our performance of pious and religious acts, may be for our own interest and for our own glory.

The "secret" intention of the work is what makes that work vanity. We may work hard, for the greatest and most noble and spiritual causes, even for God, and yet our work is mere vanity because we are really just interested in ourselves. And yet, according to Ecclesiastes, all these efforts for ourselves are in vain, because someone else is ultimately going to benefit from them.

Suppose that we work hard for our own earthly future, striving to succeed in our career, building a good reputation. Suppose also that we work hard to obtain God's blessings, to build our "holy" future, to earn our paradise. What if we discover that our future has been jeopardized? Then not only the purpose of our work will be shaken, our whole life will be shaken. If all this hard work was in vain, we have wasted our present life.

According to Ecclesiastes, this is another reason that our work is vanity: "For all his days are sorrowful, and his work grievous; even in the night his heart takes no rest. This also is vanity" (2:23). You were so concerned with the success of your life that you failed the very life you wanted to save. You worked so hard to acquire happiness that you lost happiness doing it. In the process, you missed out on the quality of life—your sleep, the enjoyment of a beautiful sunset, the sublime taste of a gourmet meal, or opportunities for deep meditation. You also suffered in the quality of your relationships—with your spouse, your children, your friends—simply because you were committed to the holy work. This failure to enjoy life for the sake of the holy work, says Ecclesiastes, is precisely what makes your holy work nothing more than vanity.

Wisdom Is Vanity

Ecclesiastes is so consistently honest that even wisdom, the very wisdom that helps him to think clearly and discern truth, is not spared. To be sure, Ecclesiastes acknowledges the superior value of wisdom: "I saw that wisdom excels folly / As light excels darkness" (2:13). this means that wisdom is supposed to help us to survive death, for darkness means death to Ecclesiastes (5:16, 17; 6:4; 11:8). If the wise person is someone whose eyes are in his head, while the fool walks in darkness (2:14), this means that the wise will survive death, the fool will not. Wisdom is regarded as the "magic" recipe to attain immortality. This was the temptation of Eve: acquire wisdom, reach the status of immortality, and be like God. This was also a common idea in ancient Egypt, where the wise man was made immortal through his words of wisdom.[2]

And yet Ecclesiastes observes that this is not the case: "The same event happens to them all" (2:14). The wise, like the fool, will die. No wonder Ecclesiastes is led to question the relevance of wisdom: "Why was I then more wise?" (2:15). He goes even so far as to question life: "Therefore I hated life" (2:17). Job had come to the same conclusion, questioning the value of his own life, after concluding that all his good works and his wisdom were of no use (Job 16:17; 3:1, 20; 10:8). Is Ecclesiastes, like Job, contemplating suicide? We don't know. What is certain, however, is that, like Job, he understood a truth that upset his original logic. Your wisdom will not save you, nor even your theological knowledge or your spiritual understanding of "the truth." Wisdom at its best will not grant you special privileges over the fool or even the wicked. You will both die. In that sense, wisdom is vanity.

The Gift of God

The discourse of Ecclesiastes started with a parable on the movements of Creation, to teach us the tragic lesson of what happened to that creation. All the "good" (tov) of the original creation by God had been supplanted by the hebel of the "not yet," the chaos of the "without form and void," identified with human work. In that context, joy, work, and wisdom are seen as vanity. But suddenly, in the conclusion of our passage (2:24–26), joy, work, and wisdom are now identified as "the gift of God." Ecclesiastes wrote, "God gives wisdom and knowledge and joy . . . He gives the work" (2:26; compare 3:13).

Joy, work, and wisdom reappear, this time in the positive context of Creation, associated with the words "good" (tov) and "to give" *(natan),* directly attributed to God. It is indeed in the context of Creation that these two words appear together and for the first time. Just like the word *good,* the word *give* is a key word of the Creation story, where it is used specifically to express the first connection between God, Creation, and the living man: "And God said, Behold, I have given you every herb bearing seed, which is upon the face of all the earth, and every tree, in the which is the fruit of a tree yielding seed; to you it shall be for meat. And to every beast of the earth, and to every fowl of the air, and to every thing that creepeth upon the earth, wherein there is life, I have given every green herb for meat: and it was so" (Genesis 1:29, 30, KJV).

Interestingly, this first association concerns food, the primary enjoyment Ecclesiastes is referring to in 2:24: "There is nothing better ["good," *tov*] for a man, than that he should eat and drink, and that his soul should enjoy good *[tov]* in his labor. This also, I saw, was from the hand of God." In that new perspective of the gift of God, in the light of Creation, the experiences of joy, work, and wisdom will take on a new meaning.

The Gift of Joy

Joy is no longer the subjective experience artificially concocted by humans to give themselves their legitimate portion of good time. It is not the fruit of a human effort, nor is it a reward we give ourselves because we deserve it. It is the gift of God. It is grace. In exalting the value of enjoyment, Ecclesiastes is not promoting the hedonist philosophy that elevates personal pleasure to the ultimate good, to the ideal of life. Rather, Ecclesiastes teaches us the value of receiving. Joy is the capacity to see what is given to us and to take it.

Ecclesiastes means, first, that we should take the gift humbly and gratefully, to learn to content ourselves with what is given to us. Without jealousy or envy, we will receive the gift of God with peace in our heart, with faith, and with hope. He is also saying that we should take the gift fully. Many religious people, indeed many Christians, are so conditioned and concerned to give that they have lost the sense of receiving. They are afraid to enjoy, ashamed to enjoy. Because of their distorted view of nature, they think it is sinful to be happy or to enjoy life. Still under the subtle influence of the Gnostic heretic Marcion (second century A.D.), many Christians see Creation, beauty, the flesh, food, and laughter as evil. For centuries Christians were taught to reject the seventh-day Sabbath, the celebration of Creation. They were encouraged instead to adopt Sunday, the day that affirmed the deliverance from Creation. Therefore, in the name of spiritual values, they have learned to despise Creation.

And this mentality has not even spared many of those who like to "keep" the seventh-day Sabbath. For some, their happiness is their deliberate rejection of happiness. The more they suffer, the more they are sad and serious, the holier they feel and thus the happier they are. In fact, this is the kind of joy Ecclesiastes calls vanity, precisely because it is a joy produced by our hands. Rather, as he puts it, it should come "from the hand of God" (2:24).

This does not mean, however, that anything is acceptable. In the perspective of joy as a gift of God, our joy is oriented and illuminated by an ethic that is also the gift of our Creator. Ecclesiastes will later elaborate on this reservation (11:9). Enjoying life is not to get drunk; it is not to abuse food or to engage in inappropriate sexual behavior. Since we receive joy from the Creator, we enjoy it as He gives it to us. Joy from His hands is joy under His control.

The Gift of Work

Work as a gift of God is no longer the hectic race for success that kills us. It is not a threatening rival that swallows our families and blurs the real reason for our work. There is an old Jewish legend about the tower of Babel that administrators of holy work ought to meditate on. The story tells us that when a brick dropped, the workers rushed to recover the precious material for the accomplishment of their sacred construction (they were building a temple). But when a man fell, they kept working, indifferent to his safety and to his life. When God saw that the workers were more concerned with the sacredness of the work than with human dignity and life, He got angry and came down to punish them.

To work for God at the expense of humans is dangerous. It leads to the *jihad* mentality and to the mindset that sparked the Crusades. Likewise this eagerness to identify ourselves with the work of God, to make it "our business," is suspect. It will ultimately lead to ethnocentrism, or nepotism and fascism, because we will believe that only those who look like us and think like us are worth having around, and that all others should be eliminated for God's cause. This was the motto of the Nazis, *Gott mit uns,* "God with us."

In the Bible, God works for the Israelites, God "fights for them" (Exodus 14:25), "lest Israel claim glory for itself" (Judges 7:2). From the Creation, to the life of Jesus, and on to scenes of the new earth, the Bible is the story of a God who works for mankind. Any attempt on our part to work for God is ridiculous and leads to nowhere; it is vanity. Work as a gift of God is a work that is received from God. Therefore it is a work conducted with passion, conviction, care, and responsibility, but also with faith, because not all depends on me.

Here again we meet the same tension of ethics and grace that characterizes the experience of the gift of God. As a gift of God, work cannot be vanity—not because it is a holy work for God but because it is God's work for me. Even if our work is not completed when Sabbath begins, we will rest anyway, trusting that God will take care of the rest. This is the main lesson contained in the Sabbath; it is a reminder of the work of God for us, His gift for mankind. The Sabbath becomes the memorial of His total grace, the moment when we should realize that He did "all" for us.

Humans were not there, working for Him, when God created all things for them; the Sabbath is the sign of this gift, a rest that we do not deserve. The irony is that sometimes those who claim to have the "truth" of the Sabbath are so zealous about it that they transform it into a busy day of doing holy works for God rather than receiving and enjoying the gift. Ecclesiastes applies this warning to such people: our work for God is vanity.

The message of Ecclesiastes contains a work ethic that would save the workaholic, the stressed, and the successful of our modern societies. Knowing that work is a gift of God will relieve the tension and eliminate the stress. Moreover, it will also save our world from poverty and hunger, for if indeed work is a gift from God, there is no reason why we should keep its fruit exclusively for ourselves. Work as a gift of God implies the duty of generosity. And even if we have amassed wealth, even if we have been successful, even if we have worked hard for it and have all the good reasons to think that we deserve it, it remains the gift of God. Therefore, it will be inappropriate to boast about it. Neither would it be appropriate to worry about it; worrying would show that we believe that all depends on our control, turning our work again into a piece of vanity.

The Gift of Wisdom

Wisdom, understood as a gift of God, is the only wisdom that is not vanity, the only real wisdom that has substance. The reason for this is quite simple and obvious: only the one who has the capacity to receive and to learn from others will be able to be wise. The ancient rabbis put it this way: "Who is wise? He who learns from all men" (*Pirke Avoth* 4, 1).

The Bible places the seat of wisdom and intelligence in the ears (Isaiah 50:5; Job 12:11; Nehemiah 8:3; compare Revelation 2:7; 3:22). The ancient Egyptians jokingly insisted that the ears of a good student were located on his back, implying that they became attentive and ready to listen as soon as they felt the staff of the master on their back.[3] Solomon defined wisdom as the capacity to hear. Asking God for wisdom, he prayed: "Give your servant an understanding [hearing][4] heart" (1 Kings 3:9). Notice that he asked for wisdom, knowing that he was not wise by himself. This attitude is already, in itself, a sign of wisdom. To be wise is to know that we are not wise by ourselves and that we need help from the outside.

According to the Biblical text, the only way to acquire this skill is through a gift from God: "I have given you a wise and understanding heart" (1 Kings 3:12). This kind of wisdom belongs to the category of revelation. It is called "the wisdom of God" (1 Kings 3:28). No wonder that wisdom is the equivalent of the "fear of the Lord" (Psalm 111:10; Proverbs 1:7). For Solomon, only this kind of wisdom, a "hearing heart" attentive to God's directions, will provide him with the ability to "discern between good and evil" (1 Kings 3:9). Any attempt to achieve wisdom apart from God will lead to the same confusion that trapped Eve, who thought, under the insidious suggestion of the serpent, that she could make it by herself and thus acquire the divine recipe. This is mankind's first and certainly most fundamental temptation, to think that we can achieve wisdom by ourselves. This temptation is not just a story of the past or an abstract theology. It is a mentality, an attitude, a way of life even. It is the illusion that we know the solution, that the kingdom of God is in our hands, that the choice between good and evil is to be determined solely by our own reasoning.

Ecclesiastes calls this wisdom vanity, for it takes us to the stage of pre-Creation, implying that Creation did not take place, that God is not the Creator. Inversely, wisdom, as a gift of God, implies that the problem of "good and evil" is in God's hands alone, that salvation is God's solution because God is the Creator. Only from the perspective of the God of Creation, the God who gives, may we be able to recover the original "good" *(tov)* that has turned into "vanity" *(hebel)*.

---

1. Note that the order putting silver before gold, showing the superior value of silver over gold is attested until the Persian period when the reverse tendency occurs (see Exodus 20:23; Deuteronomy 17:17, compare Ezekiel 16:13; Daniel 11:38, 43, etc.), suggesting that Ecclesiastes must have been written before the Persian period.

2. See Lichtheim, vol. 1, 99.

3. See Adolf Erman, *Life in Ancient Egypt* (New York: Dover Publications, 1971), 331.

4. Note that the English word "to understand" in the New King James Version is the translation of the Hebrew word *shama'* that means "to hear," "to listen" (see the note in NKJV).

CHAPTER 4

Time and Eternity

Saint Augustine of Hippo once said, "What is time? If no one asks me, I know; but if I want to explain it to a questioner, I do not know."[1] Ecclesiastes will not explain it. For him, time is not a complex abstraction that needs explanation. Time is life itself; it is the place where events happen. Unlike Greek thinking, which associated time with death, Hebrew thinking associated time with life. In Hebrew thought, time is bound up with events: There is a time for everything (Ecclesiastes 3:1).

For Ecclesiastes, it is within the flesh of our existence, here on earth, that we receive God's first gift—"time" in which the events of our life unfold. "He has made [given, *natan*] everything beautiful in its time" (3:11). Ecclesiastes also adds, in the same verse, "He has put [given, *natan*][2] eternity in their hearts" (3:11). We also receive here, in our time, a *sense* of eternity. Yet the shadow of *hebel* is spoiling the gift; the problem of evil and death breaks the harmony.

Events are both positive and negative; life stands in tension with death. So within our limited life, the gift of God obliges us to carry a double tension, between life and death, between time and eternity.

The Gift of Time

The last verses of the preceding chapter spoke about the gift of God in the context of creation. Time is the first gift of creation: " 'Let there be light'; and there was light . . . the first day" (Genesis 1:3, 5). It is also

38

significant that the first time the verb *to give* is used, it is reporting about the creation of the luminaries, which will rule over time: "God [gave *natan*] them in the firmament of the heavens to give light upon the earth, and to rule over the day and over the night, and to divide the light from the darkness. . . . the fourth day" (Genesis 1:17–19).

Ecclesiastes' first application of the lesson about the gift of God concerns "all" the times of our life. The word "all" *(kol)* is used again. But instead of being attached to vanity ("all is vanity"), it is now attached to time. The phrase "there is a time for everything *[kol]* and for every *[kol]* purpose" (see 3:1) means that every event in life has its specific moment. This text is not about ethics, as often understood. Ecclesiastes does not mean here that there are appropriate moments for people to act. These times are not operated by humans. We do not decide to die and to give birth (3:2). Nor is the text about determinism, implying that a blind fatality is striking humans in spite of and against their wills.

Instead, the message contained in this statement is that every event in life is a gift of God: "To everything there is a season" (3:1).[3] This truth is then developed in the next seven verses (3:2–8) through a beautiful song[4] that balances the opposites in seven specific rhythms:[5]

1. Birth/death;[6] plant/pluck (3:2)
2. Kill/heal; break down/build up (3:3)
3. Weep/laugh; mourn/dance (3:4)
4. Cast away stones/gather stones;[7] embrace/refrain from embracing (3:5)
5. Gain/lose; keep/throw away (3:6)
6. Tear/sew; silence/speak[8] (3:7)
7. Love/hate; war/peace (3:8).

The first thought associations, "birth/death" and "plant/pluck," immediately place us in the context of the original curse in Genesis 3:

To the woman He [God] said:
"I will greatly multiply your sorrow and your conception;
In pain you shall bring forth children . . ."
Then to Adam He said . . .
"Cursed is the ground for your sake;
In toil you shall eat of it
All the days of your life. . . .

In the sweat of your face you shall eat bread
Till you return to the ground,
For out of it you were taken;
For dust you are,
And to dust you shall return" (Genesis 3:16–19).

This poem on time must be read from the perspective of a post-Creation reflection after the fall and under the curse. According to Ecclesiastes, even these times under the curse, our times of vanity, are gifts of God.

The point of Ecclesiastes is that "all" times are given by God: not only the good times but also the bad; not only the times of life but also the times of death.

The first lesson of this statement is that God is in control of "all." There is only one God. In the context of Biblical culture, this is a strong affirmation of monotheism:

" 'Now see that I, even I, am He,
And there is no God besides Me;
I kill and I make alive;
I wound and I heal' " (Deuteronomy 32:39).

There were those who would be tempted to believe in many gods, good gods and bad ones, gods of light and gods of darkness. People with such beliefs would be dragged into polytheism, worshiping also the "powers" of darkness. To such people, the God of the Bible presents Himself as the only God:

" 'That they may know from the rising of the sun to its setting
That there is none besides Me.
I am the LORD, and there is no other;
I form the light and create darkness,
I make peace and create calamity;
I, the LORD, do all these things' " (Isaiah 45:6, 7).

Ecclesiastes speaks in that tradition.

Even today, even within our religious, monotheistic circles, there are many who divide their commitments and compromise with other gods—the god of pleasure, the god of money, the god of success. Sometimes they forget that God is also there when they sell, when they lie, when they eat, when they think that no one sees them. There are others who are so afraid of the power of evil, of Satan, that they keep talking about it and concoct a superstitious religion full of anguished precautions, amulets, and right formulas. This affirmation that God is in control of "all" is significant for them all. And the affirmation is of utmost importance for all of us, whether from an Eastern background or a Judeo-Christian one. In our confusing days, many want to please everyone and taste of every god, to make sure that they do not miss something interesting.

That God is also there in the precincts of *hebel* is an important comfort and a great assurance. Psalm 23 reminds us that He is there, even "though I walk through the valley of the shadow of death" (verse 4). He is there as a gift, concretely present; and His rod physically touches me and comforts me. God is present even when I do not feel Him, when I do not see Him, when I suffer, and when I painfully experience His silence. Isaiah tells us that this paradox is precisely the very mark of the living God, in contrast to the visible and predictable idols:

Truly You are God, who hide Yourself,
O God of Israel, the Savior! . . .
They shall go in confusion together,
Who are makers of idols (Isaiah 45:15, 16).

This incarnation of God in the midst of *hebel,* in the vanity of our lives, is the actual experience of Immanuel, "God with us." He is the God who walks with me, and who talks with me, wherever I go and whatever I do.

The regular swing of plus and minus, of happiness and pain, contains a double lesson for life. On one hand, knowing that after joy will come pain is an incentive to take advantage of the present moment of happiness and to enjoy it fully. We do not want to miss it, for it will pass. On the other hand, knowing that after pain will come joy helps us to endure the time of trouble and wait for what should come after that. The pain will not last; we learn to hope.

To believe that both kinds of time are in God's hands, that "He has made everything [the bad and the good] beautiful in its time" (3:11), helps us to trust Him in both times. It gives special meaning to those moments. For the good, the moment of happiness, it is a spiritual encouragement to welcome the gift. It adds another reason that we should enjoy it—not just because we like it and want to take advantage of it, because we feel naturally attracted to it, but also because it comes from God and is specially designed for us. To enjoy the "good" gift of God is an expression of my gratefulness towards Him.

When I taste a delicious fruit, when I smell the fragrance of a flower, when I relax in the sun, when I respond to true love, when I burst into laughter, when I discover the beautiful and feast my senses and my soul on it, I am testifying to God.

Likewise for the bad. In the moment of sorrow and trouble faith helps me believe that there is meaning and purpose in my desolation. I can be like Joseph, who saw in his affliction the hand of God, who "meant it for good, in order to bring it about as it is this day, to save many people alive" (Genesis 50:20). Or I can be like Esther, who had "come to the kingdom for such a time as this" (Esther 4:14). Or I could even be like the ancient rabbi who received the name *Gam zo le tova,* "even this is for the good," because of his faith. Whenever he got into trouble, he always responded with these words: "Even this is for the good." This phrase has been repeated by many Jews in the face of tragedy. As Paul put it, "All things work together for good" (Romans 8:28).

The Problem of Evil

This optimistic faith suggests an idyllic and harmonious picture of life, with all the times at the right place. Yet in spite of this clear principle, we know that life doesn't unfold like that. Life seems absurd, and the world unfair. In contrast with the serene faith that believes that everything has its purpose, Ecclesiastes also observes that the world is upset:

> I saw under the sun:
>
> In the place of judgment,
> Wickedness was there;
> And in the place of righteousness,
> Iniquity was there (3:16).

42

The good faith of the believer who transcends his pain by trusting God's intentions begins to wear thin. The clear and reassuring system of the good theologian, who sees meaning in everything and explains all tragedy, is suddenly shaken.

Not that Ecclesiastes contradicts himself. Nor is there another literary source that conveys another view denying the perception of faith. Ecclesiastes witnesses both. True faith does not keep us from clearly seeing the injustice and the absurdity of life. Yes, we believe that God is in control and that He is present even in the valley of darkness; but at the same time, we should recognize the evil in the world and confront it as such. Faith is not blind. On the contrary, faith implies an essential lucidity and sensitivity toward the evil in the world. Otherwise it is not faith. Faith believes in spite of what we see, not because we do not see. There are people who keep denying the reality of evil in the name of God, always singing halleluiahs and wearing an eternal smile on their lips, living in an aseptic cocoon. These pious folks do not demonstrate faith; instead, they display a weak conscience or a lack of intelligence.

"God shall judge the righteous and the wicked, / For there shall be a time there for every purpose and for every work" (3:17). Ecclesiastes makes this statement immediately after observing the problem of evil, showing that the judgment is the only appropriate response. For Ecclesiastes, however, the problem will not be addressed here on earth, during his lifetime. The "there," the place of judgment in verse 17, is located with God. It is noteworthy, indeed, that in verse 17 the word "there" *(sham)* is in parallel to "God," as this literal translation shows:

"The righteous and the wicked will judge* **God**
For (there shall be) a time for all purposes, and on all works **there**" (3:17).

(*In Hebrew, the subject follows the verb: the sentence should read as follows: "God will judge"). Also, the verb "to judge" is used in the future tense ("God will judge") and refers, therefore, to a moment in time that is clearly not taking place during the life of Ecclesiastes.

According to Ecclesiastes, the judgment will be a cosmic event. This judgment will affect "all" *(kol)*—remember, this is one of the key words of the Creation story. The word *kol* designates the whole

43

world (see chapter 1) and, therefore, has a universal application. The judgment that Ecclesiastes is referring to is not imminent. We should not hope for a solution in the course of our present existence. For Ecclesiastes the only solution to the problem of evil in the world is the cosmic solution. Because the problem of evil is cosmic in nature (Ecclesiastes had observed it "under the sun," verse 16), it needs to be addressed on a cosmic level.

This perspective has been ignored or dismissed by many who have lost the sense of God's transcendence and the awareness of the cosmic framework behind the world's problems. It is not popular to speak of the judgment of God as a specific event in time and in space, a cosmic event that should embrace the whole world. Rather, we would like to think that we should address the problem of evil ourselves, and not wait for God to do it. So far, however, as history painfully attests, we are the problem, not its solution.

To be sure, we should face our responsibility and work hard to repair the world and relieve its pain. Hunger, injustice, and crime should be handled. It is our problem. But besides this essential obligation, we should face the tragic fact of our human condition and of the condition of our world. Along with Ecclesiastes, we must realize that "what is crooked cannot be made straight," (1:15), that whatever our good intentions and our good will, the real solution to the problem of evil is not in our hands but in God's.

Just to make sure that we understand the lesson, Ecclesiastes confronts us with the absolutely unsolvable problem: cruel, clear, systematic, and nonnegotiable, death will always be there. The reference to death belongs to the same flow of thought as does the reference to the judgment. The two evocations have the same introduction, "I said in my heart" (3:17, 18), and follow each other.

The phrase "God *[ha-Elohim]* tests," in verse 18, reminds us of the phrase "God *[ha-Elohim]* shall judge," in verse 17. Both phrases apply to humans. Death and judgment pertain to the same problem of evil. Death helps us "to see" our real condition. This is what is implied in the puzzling statement, "God tests *[brr]* them, that they may see that they themselves are like beasts" (3:18). The same verb, *brr* is used in 9:1, where it is also related to the problem that the same fate strikes wicked and righteous, the problem of evil *(ra'):* "This is an evil in all that is done under the sun: that one thing happens *[qarah]* to all. . . . they go to the dead" (9:3). In 3:19 the evil is that death "happens" *(qarah)* to men and beasts.

This time, though, the evil is described simply as vanity. We have already heard the same irony in regard to the fool and the wise. They will both die (2:15, 16); there also death is described as vanity. The wise and the fool (chapter 2), the wicked and the righteous (chapter 9), and humans and beasts (chapter 3) will all die. But in our passage the absurdity of the evil is more dramatic because it associates humans and beasts under the same fate. We humans, along with chickens and goats, will all die. There is no appeal from this judgment, and there is no second opinion.

Now, the death Ecclesiastes has in mind is not a false death. The "spirit" that resides in humans is of the same nature as the one that resides in the beasts: "They all have one breath *[ruach]*" (3:19). In Hebrew, the word *ruach,* "spirit," means also "breath" or "air." In fact, for Ecclesiastes, "breath" is nothing but the vapor of vanity *(hebel).* He makes that connection through a play on words: "All have one breath . . . all is vanity" (3:19). There is no room here for the popular idea of the immortality of the soul. "All go to one place: all are from the dust, and all return to dust" (3:20). And when Ecclesiastes asks the question, "Who knows the spirit *[ruach]* of the sons of men, which goes upward, and the spirit *[ruach]* of the beast, which goes down to the earth?" (3:21), he is not suggesting a favored treatment for humans.

On the contrary, he probably has in mind the ancient Egyptian belief that after death some kind of spiritual entity (the *ba*) flew to the gods in heaven. He is then asking a rhetorical question, implying the same fate for both. This is just what he said in the preceding verse. And he is speaking the same way in the next verse: "Who can bring him to see what will happen after him?" (3:22).

For Ecclesiastes, the dead end of death is an important argument to show the absurd vanity of our human condition. There is nothing after death. Therefore, "all is vanity."

The Sense of Eternity

The only way out of this tragic and hopeless condition is another gift of God: "Also He has put eternity in their hearts" (3:11). In addition to the gift of time, the gift of this existence of vanity, God "gives eternity." The same word *natan,* "to give," is used for both gifts. The gift of eternity is in fact an intensification of the gift of time. Eternity does not take us outside of time but, rather, elevates us to a super-time. Eternity is not the end of time; rather, it is a time that has no end. This means that eternity will always be provided with new events. Biblical hope implies the absolute new. It is the creation of new heavens and a new earth (Isaiah 65:17; compare Revelation 21:1, 2). Eternity is characterized by the intensification of new times. In eternity, time is therefore more present than ever.

But this experience of eternity, absolute in quantity and in quality, is foreign to our present situation. Rather, Ecclesiastes says that eternity is given only in the heart. It is not an actual experience that is lived here within our time of vanity. We have only a *sense* of eternity. It is an experience beyond human comprehension.[9] Eternity is essentially a divine quality, in stark contrast to our humanity.

God is called "the Eternal God," *'El 'olam* (Genesis 21:33, NIV). Ecclesiastes specifically associates eternity with God: "Whatever God does, / It shall be forever" (3:14). God's work has an eternal quality; it cannot be broken: "Nothing can be added to it, / And nothing taken from it" (3:14).

This is the opposite of the human order. In the human order, we cannot repair because the human order is forever broken (1:15), while in the divine order we cannot repair because the divine order is forever perfect. This is why Ecclesiastes comments, "That which is has already been, / And what is to be has already been" (3:15). Since the work of God is perfect, it is eternal; it was in the past and will forever be. The same formula, which was used in 1:10 to depict human powerlessness toward time, our inability to achieve anything new, is now applied to God to affirm that He controls time. Past and future are in His hands. God catches "what is pursued"[10] (3:15). The Hebrew verb *radaf,* translated as "pursued," implies something that is always fleeing, impossible to catch. It refers to the elusive quality of eternity. In Psalm 23, the same verb is used to describe the eternal presence of goodness and mercy in the kingdom of God: "Surely goodness and mercy shall follow *[radaf]* me / . . . Forever" (Psalm 23:6). Eternity is with God. The gift of eternity in the human heart should, then, originate with God, who gives what He has.

That God has given us eternity in our heart means, then, that we have received a sense of another reality, of another order—the reality and order of God. This means, first of all, that as human beings we have a perception of something that is other than what we actually know, other than what we have and are. In spite of our limited mortal nature, we have the capacity to think about the infinite and eternal God. Only God could have been able to perform this delicate heart operation.

Ironically, even those who question His very existence possess that bold sense of something else—when they dream of a world of justice and peace while living in a world that has never known justice and peace; when they have a longing for the sublime in the mediocrity of their existence; when they sing what cannot be expressed in words; when they shape a masterpiece of art out of a secret image hidden in their heart.

Indeed we all sense eternity within our time of vanity and misery. It is this special moment of happiness that has taken us beyond the borders of time. It is this special holy time, this Sabbath, that brings the taste of eternity, time that speaks of freedom and of full life. But it is only a sense, a spark. We do not have eternity. We can only think or dream about it. We can only hope.

---

1. *Confessions*, XI, sec. XIV.

2. The Hebrew word *natan* means "to give." NKJV has it translated "to put."

3. This is clearly indicated by the preposition *to,* the *lamed* denoting the genitive, attached to the word *all* (3:15).

4. This text inspired the song "Turn, Turn, Turn!" (To Everything There Is a Season) written by Pete Seeger in the 1950s and interpreted later by McGuinn's famous rock board, The Byrds, in 1965 and then by country music singer, Dolly Parton, in 1984, and again in 2005. I am endebted to Gary Krause for this information.

5. The "distich" is a group of two lines bringing a complete sense.

6. Note that the opposite of death is not life but birth, referring here to the two poles, which make the two extremities of existence; birth that opens to life in contrast to death that closes life.

7. The image of throwing and gathering stones had a sexual connotation in the ancient Near East (see L. Levy, *Das Buch Qohelet* [Leipzig: Hinrich's, 1912], 81.); compare Exodus 1:16; Jeremiah 2:27; Matthew 3:9. See also the ancient Jewish commentary *Qohelet Rabbah,* which takes the gathering of the stones as sexual intercourse and the casting of the stones as continence, in parallel to embracing, and refraining from embracing.

8. The reference to tearing and sewing alludes to the mourning practices and, therefore, parallels the times of silence and speaking (see *Qohelet Rabbah*).

9. The Hebrew word *'olam* for *eternity* is derived from the root *'lm,* meaning "to hide"; significantly, the word appears in parallel with *str* (Job 28:21), from which comes our word *mystery.*

10. The text of NKJV translates "what is past", but the verb literally means "what is pursued" (see the note of NKJV).

The Other

Ecclesiastes moves from theology to ethics. From abstract thinking about the great metaphysical problems of joy and work, life, death, eternity, and evil, Ecclesiastes "returns" (Ecclesiastes 4:1) now to "under the sun," to the world of "vanity" (3:16).

Again he is confronted with evil. He is no longer having a spiritual conversation with his heart. Just as in 3:16, Ecclesiastes sees evil. But this time, what he sees is not evil in general as an abstraction, as in 3:16–21 (wickedness and death). Now the evil he sees comes in the physical and historical form of the "other" person. The harm is inflicted by the other. The numeral two or the word *second* is repeated seven times in chapter four,[1] a stylistic way to emphasize the presence of the other.

This notion is already a lesson by itself. It is important that the professionals of wisdom, the students of Torah, the theologians, and the philosophers leave the quietness of their room and the high world of ideas and plant themselves within the human reality. Apart from humanness, holiness and wisdom are neither holy nor wise. However profound their truths may be, if it is no more than a spiritual or intellectual exercise, it may well degenerate into irrelevant propositions or a dangerous delirium. Wisdom and holiness must be tied to our humanity and humanness.

For Ecclesiastes, the two worlds of wisdom and humanness are in touch with each other and inform each other. The principle of "vanity" that Ecclesiastes had developed at a theological level is now applied to the dynamic experience with the other. Ecclesiastes sees vanity in four situations that imply the other person, four pairs of individuals: (1) being under ("in the hand of") the other, (2) against the other, (3) with or without the other, and (4) in the place of the other. Each situation is regularly marked with the same phrase that directly involves Ecclesiastes' attention, according to an alternate sequence: "I returned" (4:1), "I saw" (4:4), "I returned" (4:7), "I saw" (4:15). Each time Ecclesiastes draws the lesson of what is "good." The instruction is given in the form of proverbs to make it more catchy and memorable, and also to make it more universal.

The Tears of the Oppressed

The first face of the other person has tears on it. These are not tears of the one who mourns or of the one who feels an emotion. They are tears caused by the actions of the other. One can hear this already in the sound of the Hebrew words, where "the tears of the oppressed" and the parallel phrase "in the hand of the oppressors" echo each other.[2] Likewise, the word "oppressed" is in the passive form. The "oppressed" has no initiative of his own. He does not exist by himself, but is in the hands of the oppressor. He is the perfect victim.

The identity of the victim and the nature of the oppression are not given. Every victim is encompassed by this intentional anonymity, and not just the victims of political or economic oppression, those who died in the gas chambers or the killing fields. These faceless victims are the oppressed women in private homes and in the office, the oppressed children in the drunkard's house or in the boarding school, the oppressed prisoner in jail, the oppressed soldier in the barracks. It includes all who have suffered at the hands of others.

The word *oppress* occurs three times, suggesting the intensity of that oppression. This is a perfect oppression in which the oppressor has all the power. No resistance is registered. Nothing stands in the way of the oppressor. There is no one to help the victim. This observation, more than anything, shocks Ecclesiastes. The phrase "they have no comforter" (4:1) is repeated twice. The phrase is loaded with special meaning because here Ecclesiastes alludes to God.

Indeed, saying that "they have no comforter" is to suggest the absence of God. This exact phrase is used in the book of Lamentations with the same meaning.[3] There the prophet Jeremiah deplores the fact that the Israelites "have no comforter" (Lamentations 1:2, 9, 17, 21). He cries precisely because God, who was supposed to be their comforter, is not there:

"For these things I weep;
My eye, my eye overflows with water;
Because the comforter, who should restore my life,
Is far from me" (Lamentations 1:16).

In biblical tradition, God is called "the Comforter" (Isaiah 51:12; 66:13). One classic text that represents God as the comforter is Psalm 23: "You are with me; / Your rod and Your staff, they comfort me" (verse 4).

Ecclesiastes is thus confronted with an unbearable reality, the absence of God, which Martin Buber has called "the eclipse of God."[4] And since God is absent, Ecclesiastes praises the void. The verb "to praise" *(shabach),* which always applies to God,[5] is here applied to "the dead" (4:2) whom Ecclesiastes has just identified as "dust" (3:20), nothing. It is as if the sky above Ecclesiastes was empty. God is not responding.

The whole theological system of Ecclesiastes is shaken. Didn't he assure us that God was present even in pain? Didn't he teach us that the time of suffering as well as the time of joy is a gift of God? Now he seems to suggest the contrary. The vision of the absolute violence of the oppression and the tears of the oppressed affects his theology and his religious behavior. Even his prayer has changed. He is angry with God and shouts into the void.

One who has never seen or who has refused to see the horror of oppression and the tears of the oppressed will not resonate with Ecclesiastes. He will keep thinking the same way, intellectually but insensitively, as if nothing has happened. His theology, his reading of the Bible, will not be affected by tragedy. But is this aseptic theology worthy to be called theology? German theologian Johann Baptist Metz had this question in mind when he gave this solemn warning: "What Christian theologians can do for the murder of Auschwitz . . . is this: Never again to do theology in such a way that its construction remains unaffected or could remain unaffected by Auschwitz."[6] Ecclesiastes' theology would have been affected by Auschwitz, so much so that when he sees the radical evil, he questions the sense of life, that very life that is God's gift: "Better than both (the living and the dead) is he who has never existed, / Who has not seen the evil work that is done under the sun" (4:3).

Ecclesiastes is not the only one in the Bible to have had his theology shaken in the face of tragedy. In the book of Job, the wise man, who also happens to be the victim, challenges God and questions the sense of life: "May the day perish on which I was born" (Job 3:3), "Why did I not die at birth?" (Job 3:11), and "Why is light given to him who is in misery?" (Job 3:20).

Was Job's theology worthy? Certainly not for the good theologians of that time (Job's three visitors) who defended their traditional system, thinking that they were defending God. Yet at the end of the story, we learn God's evaluation of this aseptic theology: "My wrath is aroused against you and your two friends, for you have not spoken of Me what is right, as My servant Job has" (Job 42:7). The paradox is that the one who shouted at God and questioned the sense of life in the face of misery was closer to God than those who defended Him and sought to preserve their serene and rational theology.

It is significant that both books, Job and Ecclesiastes, with all their disturbed and disturbing reflections, were accepted into the biblical canon. This tells us that it is all right, even required, to shout at God and revolt at the pain in the world, and to stand with the oppressed. For only then are you near to God.

It's a great paradox. At that very moment, when Ecclesiastes is having a problem with God because of the tears of the oppressed, when he feels that his skies are empty, in this apparent absence of God, Ecclesiastes has never been so close to God, and God has never been so present.

This paradoxical presence of God in His absence is suggested through a subtle literary echo. The repetition of the phrase "they have no comforter . . . they have no comforter" (4:1) reminds us of another dramatic repetition: "wickedness was there . . . [wickedness] was there" (3:16). The two passages are hinting at each other. Wickedness was there where righteousness was expected, just as the comforter was not there where He was expected. We remember that on the horizon of 3:16 loomed the prospect of a cosmic judgment, which will address the cosmic problem of evil and restore righteousness. The double sigh of Ecclesiastes, "they have no comforter . . . they have no comforter," is paradoxically pregnant with hope. Ecclesiastes has just given us a lesson about the structure of hope. We learn to hope only when we are confronted with the pain of the world, only when we see evil as it is.

The Hands of the Fool

The "second" in this chapter, the "other," does not show any face. The focus is on the hands: folded hands (4:5), open palms, and closed fists (4:6). The scenario of a conflict is suggested through those hands. On one side, we see closed and tense hands, which shift from "folded" to "grasping." On the other side, we see one open and relaxed hand, which is quiet. The cause of the conflict is given in the introduction of the passage: "envy" (4:4).

The story is about the lazy person, described with folded hands (Proverbs 6:10). He doesn't do anything; his hands are occupied only with themselves. Then envy comes. The lazy person will become wicked, because he will end up desiring and coveting and consequently grasping for what he does not have, but what the other does. The two steps are indicated through two proverbs following each other. Although these two proverbs appear separately in the book of Proverbs,[7] here, they are put together, suggesting that they are to be read in connection. Indeed, in our passage, verse 6 is the explicit commentary of verse 5; it explains the mechanism of passing from laziness to envy and then to wickedness.

In biblical tradition, envy is associated with oppression and wickedness. Joseph was persecuted by his brothers because they envied him (Genesis 37:11). Jesus was sent to the cross "because of envy" (Matthew 27:18). Even the violent conflicts of Israel were related to envy (Isaiah 11:13). It is also noteworthy that in the book of Proverbs envy is listed next to the oppressor and the wicked: "Envy is rottenness to the bones. / He who oppresses the poor. . . . / The wicked is banished" (Proverbs 14:30, 31, 32).

Ecclesiastes tells us that envy leads to nowhere and is counterproductive, predicting that the lazy man will eventually "consume his own flesh" (4:5). How ironic, considering that he was envious of the other's belonging. The lesson, then, of Ecclesiastes is that it is better to have less with peace than to have more with a conflict that leads, ultimately, to self-destruction and having empty hands.

From this observation, Ecclesiastes draws his lesson about vanity. Not only is the move of the lazy man in vain, it is also ridiculous. He ends up working hard because he insisted on being lazy. Even his laziness is in vain. He did not want to give of himself, and the result is that he will eat himself. He wanted to enjoy himself at the expense of the other, and the result is his own suffering.

The parable Nathan the prophet told to David about the little ewe lamb of the poor man (2 Samuel 12:1–15) comes to mind. Just as the rich man took the poor man's lamb rather than taking one from his own flock, King David took the wife of Uriah the Hittite and killed her husband. David paid a high price for this iniquity. His reign suffered constant adversity, and the child, the fruit of this adulterous union, died.

Certainly the story was still vivid in Solomon's memory. The ewe lamb of the poor man was Bathsheba, Solomon's mother. It is quite possible that Ecclesiastes alludes to that painful incident. The envy reminds him of the king who coveted the other's wife. The folding of the hands reminds us of the king who chose not to take from his own flock. The closed fists and the violent stripping of the poor remind us of the king who stole the woman and had her husband killed. And the similar tragic result, the grasping of the wind, brings to mind the death of the child born of the adulterous union. Ecclesiastes' satire may well apply to Solomon himself, too, who "raised forced labor" (1 Kings 9:21) and abused his power (1 Kings 12:4).

But the parable of Ecclesiastes is more than just an exercise of memory or an autobiography. It contains a series of ethical lessons that transcend time. First is the sterile nature of envy—the desire to put your hand on what does not belong to you will make your hands empty. Second, the foolishness of laziness—if you want to be lazy because you dislike work, you will work even harder and in vain. Third, the anguish of greediness—it is better to be happy with less than miserable with more. And finally, the fruit of the mistake—

sooner or later our iniquity comes back to us like a boomerang. In essence, all these lessons are teaching us that trying to take advantage of the other does not profit in anything. It is vanity.

The Friends and the Lonely

The two previous cases had confirmed the truth of the Italian proverb "Better to be alone than in bad company." In the light of these experiences, we would be tempted indeed to flee mankind. "The more I see humans," deplored a humorist, "the more I love my dog."

Yet Ecclesiastes does not go there. Even this option is vanity, says Ecclesiastes: "This also is vanity and a grave misfortune" (literally, "an evil task," 4:8). So, Ecclesiastes pleads the opposite view: "Two are better than one" (4:9). The greatest concentration of the word *two* is in that passage, five occurrences, against six occurrences of the word *one*. Ecclesiastes proves his point in two systematic steps. First, he shows us the inconvenience of being alone (4:8); then, he displays the advantage of being in company (4:9–12).

Staying alone is vanity, argues Ecclesiastes, because there is no one, no companion, no brother, and no son to share with. It is essentially the absence of the other that makes our life vanity. In the absence of others, we concentrate only on inanimate objects. We see only things. But our eye is never "satisfied with riches" (4:8). We will never know the value and the joy of life because we are depriving ourselves of "good" *(tov)*, the very characteristic of creation. Ecclesiastes considers this situation "evil" *(ra')*, the opposite of "good."

It belongs, therefore, to anticreation; it is *hebel*. It does not exist. Verse 8 is full of negations (four times). Selfishness empties us of existence and dehumanizes us. Being alone, we lose the sense of who we are or even that we are.

The story of the creation of the first man in Genesis 2 suggests this vital lesson. When all the animals pass before Adam, the biblical text tells us that he gives them a name. But the text reports no words coming out of Adam's mouth. No wonder God got worried and gave this diagnosis: "It is not good *[tov]* that man should be alone" (Genesis 2:18). It is that same "good" that Ecclesiastes sees missing in the lonely man.

The first time Adam really spoke was when Eve was introduced to him.

Adam said:
"This is now bone of my bones
And flesh of my flesh;
She shall be called Woman,
Because she was taken out of Man" (Genesis 2:23).

Before this confrontation, Adam could not have known who he was; his only points of reference were the ox and the goat. To the existential question Who am I? Adam would not have been able to answer. Adam became human only when the other came along. Before that crucial moment, we may even wonder if he would have been able to ask the question. For Ecclesiastes, the answer is clear. The lonely "never asks" (4:8). He is so taken by his work and so focused on the object that he forgets to be.

The situation of being "two," on the other hand, is identified as "good" (tov). The word tov is repeated twice in the introductory verse (4:9). The existence of the "two" is now given in contrast to the nonexistence of the "one" of verse 8: the phrase "there is [yesh] reward for . . . their labor" (4:9) is in contrast to the phrase "there is no [eyn] end to his labors" (4:8).

Three adverse circumstances are given to support the argument that "two are better than one": when we stumble (4:10), when we are cold (4:11), and when we fight (4:12). It is interesting that Ecclesiastes does not refer to the beauty or the value of friendship, or of love, to make his point. He does not embarrass himself with emotion or abstract principles. His focus is on life. The three circumstances are matters of bare survival. When we fall, we help each other; when we are cold in the night, we warm each other; and when we are threatened by a common enemy, we fight together against him. The reason for this neutral tone is that Ecclesiastes thinks in general terms. This observation should apply to any two, whether they are lovers, friends, or simply colleagues.

The poem concludes with a proverb, "a threefold cord is not quickly broken" (4:12). The commentaries warn us that we should not be literalistic about the number three, as it relates to the two friends, suggesting that it simply means plurality. But the three versus the two may well be intentional. When we are two, we encourage ourselves and our force is multiplied, so that we may indeed feel as three. Also, being two may generate a third one: a child, or simply the friend of the friend, for the friend of the friend is also my friend.

At any rate, the idea is that we should not be alone; man is essentially a social being and will survive and learn to be himself only in relationship, within the community. It is noteworthy that the Hebrew word for "man," (*'ish*),[8] the very word that is used in the context of Genesis 2, implies this social dimension. It is interesting that in the Bible, God's covenant and salvation always concern the community. And when it seems to involve the individual, Abraham or Jacob, for instance, it is always in relation to the whole people, the future people of Israel for the latter, and all the nations for the former.

God reveals Himself at Sinai to a people. In the New Testament, He calls the *ekklesia,* "the church," as part of His covenant. In Judaism, the community is a prerequisite for worship. We need the *minyan,* a minimum of ten, to pray. Even eschatological salvation, the ultimate act of God to bring us to His kingdom of peace and justice, concerns a community. It is not a private villa, or a personal encounter, but a city, the place of the community par excellence, "the New Jerusalem" (Revelation 21:2). We exist, we are saved, within the community and not apart from it, for salvation is not an individual, private affair. It has a cosmic character.

Indeed, "no man is an island," as poet John Donne[9] put it, but also "religion is not an island," as Abraham Heschel echoed.[10] This is why mission is so important and such a coherent implication. From the biblical perspective, revelation and the adventure with God cannot proceed alone. Reaching out to the other, or joining the community, is a subsequent step to the religious commitment.

The Poor Man and the King

The fourth other is not seen as a physical person. The first has tears, the second has hands, and the third has eyes. The fourth is qualified only for what he is, a poor but wise young man, or a foolish old king. On one hand, the details of the scenario are too specific to apply to a universal situation: a poor young man who happens to be wise and popular comes out of prison to become king, replacing an old and senile king. Although he is wise and young, the successor will not satisfy "those who come afterward" (4:16). Ecclesiastes concludes that "this also is vanity."

This portrayal fits well the story of Solomon's succession. The successor of the king in Ecclesiastes' parable corresponds to Jeroboam, who was the son of a widow (1 Kings 11:26); therefore, presumably he was poor. Jeroboam was also young and noted for his skills (1 Kings 11:28). He was also known for his rebellion against the king, which obliged him to flee and take refuge in Egypt (1 Kings 11:28–40). From this captivity, he returned to become king after Solomon, taking the throne to rule the majority of the people, the ten tribes of Israel (1 Kings 11:35). The king in the parable corresponds to Solomon, who lost his wisdom and his loyalty to God when he became old (1 Kings 9:4–8).

It is interesting that Solomon describes himself in the same terms, as a fool (1:17; 2:3, 9, 10). This self-criticism is a sign that Solomon repented and had learned the lessons of his foolishness. The sad end and aftermath of the parable, "those who come afterward will not rejoice" (4:16), also fits the case of Jeroboam, who became for following generations the symbol of sin against God and his people (1 Kings 15:34; 16:2, 19, 26; 22:52).

Did Solomon simply use his keen mind to guess the future? After all, he personally knew Jeroboam and could already have discerned the potential damage. Or did he prophesy? In any case, the passage of Ecclesiastes sounds like a prophetic oracle with its cosmic language—the repetition of the key word "all" *(kol)*, the use of the technical term "end" *(qets)*—often used in prophetic contexts,[11]— and the use of the future tense.

Whatever the case, the lesson of vanity remains the same. The story started with an aphorism that no one would contest: "Better is a poor and wise youth / Than an old and foolish king" (4:13). Better the young and brilliant Jeroboam, even though he is poor, than the old fool, even though he is king. "Not so fast!" says the old fool, ironically. But if you look at what comes afterward, the final product, the wise young man did not do better: "Surely this also is vanity and grasping for the wind" (4:16).

The future is the best test of all; only the result, the end of the way, will tell if our way was vanity or not. This is the perspective of Ecclesiastes as he faced the tears of the oppressed, the folded-handed fool, the lonely man, and now the one who takes the throne. All scenarios are tested and found to be vanity in the light of the future. And thus, Ecclesiastes is teaching hope.

In the previous chapter, the lesson of hope was shaped out of the spark of eternity and the little times of joy. From these we learned to imagine, to sense the better, and foretaste the kingdom; we learned to hope. In this chapter, the lesson of hope has been forced out of the negative confrontation with evil, oppression, envy, selfishness, and failure. From them we have learned to discern the vanity of present life and to feel the need for another kingdom. So hope springs from a combination of both lessons, from the good and the bad. The good gives us the sense of something else, and the bad awakens in us the need for something else.

---

1. Four times "two" (*shnayim*; verses 3, 9, 11, 12) and three times "second" (*sheny*; verses 8, 10, 15).

2. The Hebrew text shows a repetition of consonant sounds: *dim'at ha'ashuqim* ("the tears of the oppressors") // *umiyad 'oshqeyhem* ("from the hand of their oppressors"). This literary device is called an alliteration. Note also the syntactical parallelism between the two phrases: both begin with a singular collective (literally, "the tear" // "the hand") and both end with a plural ("oppressors").

3. The same grammatical form of the expression (with another verb) is used in Psalm 22 to describe the forsaking by God: "there is none to help" (Psalm 22:11), a phrase that will also be used in the book of Daniel to express the same idea. See Daniel 11:45; compare 8:4, 7 and 9:26, where it applies to the forsaking by God of the Messiah (compare Jacques Doukhan, *The Mystery of Israel* [Hagerstown, Md.: Review and Herald®, 2004], 36–38.)

4. Martin Buber, *The Eclipse of God: Studies in the Relation Between Religion and Philosophy* (New York: Harper, 1952).

5. See Psalm 117:1; 106:47; 147:12; 1 Chronicles 16:35.

6. J. B. Metz, "Christians and Jews after Auschwitz," in *A Holocaust Reader: Responses to the Nazi Extermination* (New York: Oxford University Press, 2001), 246.

7. See Proverbs 6:10 (compare 24:33) and 15:16, 17 (compare 16:8).

8. The word probably derives from the root *'nsh*, meaning "weak" and "dependent."

9. *Meditation* XVII.

10. "No Religion Is an Island," *Union Seminary Quarterly Review* 21, no. 2, pt. 1 (1966).

11. The word "end," is mostly used in the book of Daniel: 15 occurrences of the Hebrew word, *qets,* out of 67 in the whole Bible, of which 3 are in Ecclesiastes (see 4:8, 16; 12:17), and 7 occurrences of the Hebrew/Aramaic word, *sof,* out of 10 in the whole Bible, of which 3 are in Ecclesiastes (see 3:11; 7:2; 12:13).

CHAPTER 6

Religion, Power, and Money

Ecclesiastes has been speaking in the first person, sharing general principles of ethics. Now he moves on to admonitions, addressed in the second person singular to an indefinite audience. The admonitions that follow may apply to his pupil, to his son, or to all of us.

Ecclesiastes' tone has changed. He utters ten imperative phrases: "Walk prudently" (literally, keep your feet!) (Ecclesiastes 5:1); "draw near to hear" (5:1); "do not be rash with your mouth" (5:2); "let not your heart utter anything hastily" (5:2); "let your words be few" (5:2); "do not delay to pay" (5:4); "do not let your mouth . . . sin" (5:6); do not say (5:6); "fear God" (5:7); "do not marvel" (5:8).

It is not enough for us to know what is right; we have to live right. Before the time of Karl Marx, Friedrich Nietzsche, and Michel Foucault, Ecclesiastes took under his scrutiny the three driving forces of life—religion, power, and money—and warned us against them.

The Vanity of Religion

Ecclesiastes opens his exhortation with the deception of religion. The first imperative is a technical religious term, "Keep!" *(shamor)*, which is normally used in relation to the commandments (Deuteronomy 6:17; 11:22; 27:1). This is the verb connected to the Sabbath commandment (Deuteronomy 5:12). Here, the verb concerns the fundamental act of religion, "go[ing] to the house of God" (5:1). Ecclesiastes warns us that we have to "keep our feet," to be careful, when we go to the presence of God. It is obvious that we cannot go to meet God in the same way that we go for a walk or go shopping. The immediate meaning of this warning is to make us aware of the sacredness of the movement.

In the context of wisdom literature, the expression *keep the foot* means to be careful not to stumble (Proverbs 3:26). We could stumble even when we practice religion and "do evil" without even knowing it (5:1). This is what Ecclesiastes calls "the sacrifice of fools." The Bible records several cases, such as Cain (Genesis 4:1–9), Saul (1 Samuel 13:1–15), and Solomon (1 Kings 11:7–9) himself had done evil while offering sacrifices.

But Ecclesiastes is not referring to the wrong sacrifice or to the wrong religion. Even when going to the right church, even when making all the right moves, we may be making "the sacrifice of fools." Ecclesiastes gives two specific examples of this mishap.

The first example has to do with the "words" (5:2, 3) we pronounce before God, the exercise of prayer. We should not rush with our mouth, says Ecclesiastes; we should control our language. Although our words come from our heart, not everything is appropriate when we speak to God. Praying requires thinking and paying attention. In our culture of intense communication and mass media, words have lost their weight. Words are often said without much thought. Likewise, our prayers have lost meaning, not carrying the force of real prayer anymore. Too often the words of our prayers are designed to be on display and be admired by others. We are gratified to hear someone say, "What a beautiful prayer!" after we have said "Amen."

Frequently the words of our prayers are mechanical, recited without thought. We don't even understand what we are saying, or we forget that we have just prayed. And sometimes our prayers are incoherent, symptoms of our own foolishness.

Ecclesiastes indicates the reason for these problems: we are no longer praying to God. We have lost the sense of the distance of God, that He is in heaven and we are on earth. So we are praying to a god of our own measure, an idol that is not listening. Or we are just talking to ourselves. Ecclesiastes advises: "Therefore, let your words be few." It is better to say a few meaningful words, expressing careful thought, than to utter a multitude of empty words that do not go beyond the ceiling. Ecclesiastes compares these words to "dreams," which in the context of the ancient Near East, and particularly in ancient Egypt, were considered as a figure for things that are fleeting and illusory and even deceptive.[1] For Ecclesiastes, dreams are something like *hebel*, "vanity"; the two words appear together in 5:7 as synonyms.

Many religious persons ought to listen to Ecclesiastes' advice. Jesus made the same recommendation: " 'When you pray, do not use vain repetitions as the heathen do. For they think that they will be heard for their many words' " (Matthew 6:7). And yet, many Jews and many Christians still believe that the longer their prayer is, the greater its value. Whether a recitation of the endless rosary, a hastily read passage from a prayer book, or the public reading of a prepared prayer inflicted on the patient churchgoers, it is the same syndrome that Ecclesiastes and Jesus are concerned about.

The second example has to do with "vows" (5:4, 5), when we make promises to God, or in God's presence, and do not fulfill them. The book of Proverbs refers to this behavior: "It is a snare for a man to devote rashly something as holy, / And afterward to reconsider his vows" (Proverbs 20:25). The principle underlying this warning is rooted in God's covenant with His people. Our commitment to fulfill our promises to God is a response to Him. But our good intentions stumble on the weakness of our nature. We are bound to fail in our commitment to God. This is why, in Jewish tradition, the Day of Atonement has been associated not only with the forgiveness of all our sins but also with the cancellation of our vows, as the Jewish prayer *Kol Nidrey*[2] reminds us. The Bible assures us that God has forgiven us and that everyone is now free from their debt toward God. This is the implicit promise of the Lord's Prayer: " 'Forgive us our debts' " (Matthew 6:12). God's mercy overcomes His justice.[3]

The point of Ecclesiastes, however, is not so much our failure to fulfill the vow as it is our honesty toward God, the lightness of our words, and the fact that we do not take God seriously. Even if we believe that God is merciful enough to forgive us, the problem remains. It is still preferable not to make vows than to make them hastily, without thinking, and then retract them when we realize the implication of our words. And the assurance of God's forgiveness does not lighten the gravity of the case. Also, the vows that are targeted here are not so much the important vows, the ones to serve God or to remain faithful to our spouse; those important commitments do not belong to the category of Ecclesiastes' vows and are taken care of in other contexts.

What Ecclesiastes has in mind is the multiplication of pious words and wishes to do something for God that are never actualized and therefore end up being *lies*. The idea of *lie* is in fact implied in that warning; the Hebrew word *chabal,* for "destroy" (5:6), is associated with the word *lies* (see Isaiah 32:7). In the same category are all the little lies we commit in connection with God—all the virtuous actions we boast about but that never take place, all the fancy witnesses of miracles we tell to show off our religious superiority, all the "pious" lies we use to prove God in our apologetic zeal. For Solomon all these false vows for God, all these lies in connection to God, are often spoken for the personal benefit of the religious person, perhaps for his own glory. These are nothing but vanity and will lead to destruction.

Ecclesiastes has urged us from the beginning of his admonition "to draw near to hear rather than to give" (5:1). There lies precisely the vanity of religion. We are eager to give and to work for God rather than to hear and to receive from Him. This is what Ecclesiastes keeps saying: human works lead nowhere; they are vanity. And when it comes to religion, to pious works and intentions, it is even worse because we claim to achieve them on behalf of the great God of Creation, the one who gives everything. The result is this ridiculous and empty gift, "the sacrifice of fools."

We may fool ourselves, but we cannot fool God. It is significant that this section closes with the injunction to "fear God" (5:7). The same admonition is found in the conclusion of the whole book. There, God is presented as the judge: "Fear God. . . . / For God will bring every work into judgment" (12:13, 14). To "fear God" means to be aware that God is the judge; He not only tests the vanity of our religion, He also judges the earth.

The Vanity of Power

Now, if we do not see justice and righteousness on this earth, we should not be surprised (5:8). The reason, according to Ecclesiastes, lies in the principle that there is always another power above every power, with the earth being the power superior over all; even the king must submit to the land. The Hebrew word *yitron*, translated as "profit" in the phrase "the profit of the land is for all" (5:9), means "superiority" and is used to signify the superiority of light over darkness (2:13), or the superiority of wisdom over foolishness (7:12; 10:10). This meaning fits our context, rising to a crescendo of "superiority": the superiority of "a high official" over another "high official," and the superiority of "higher officials . . . over them" (5:8), and finally the "superiority" ("the profit") of the land over all (5:9). Even "the king himself is served from the field" (5:9).

Our passage makes reference to two other biblical contexts: Genesis 2 and 3, which speak about the working of the land (Genesis 2:5) by man and the curse of the earth (Genesis 3:17, 18); and 1 Chronicles 29:10–15, which reports David's prayer before anointing Solomon as king (compare verses 21, 22). Both of these texts share with our passage a number of common words and associations.

In Genesis chapters 2 and 3, as in Ecclesiastes 5, we find the same words "earth," "land," and "serve." The connection with the first two chapters of Genesis takes us into the context of the curse of the earth and the dependence of man on the land. As famous Jewish commentator Rashi explains: "For though he is a king, he is the subject to the field; if it produces fruit, he can eat, if not, he will die of hunger."[4] This connection suggests the reason for the lack of justice: we are under the curse, and there is no way we can avoid that tragic implication of evil.

In 1 Chronicles 29, we find the words *over all* (verses 11, 12), and *earth* (verses 11, 15) in common with Ecclesiastes 5. This connection takes us into the context of David's prayer, which underlines God's sovereignty: "You are exalted as head over all" (verse 11), "You reign over all" (verse 12), "all things come from You" (verse 14). It is noteworthy that the word *all* (*kol*) is used ten times in the prayer. This emphasis suggests that above "all" these powers of wickedness, which are the result of the curse, God rules. The Judge is over all of them. We do not see Him, He is not mentioned, yet He is behind all. He is present, even though He seems to be absent.

Ecclesiastes speaks the language of hope. At the same time, we are reminded that, apart from this assurance of God's sovereignty, the race for "power" leads nowhere, except to vanity. Ironically, the ambitious person who loves power will always be the subject of someone. The race is endless. And when we think we have reached the top, like a king, we realize that even there we are mere servants. "We serve the field," and our new master is blind and under the curse. This is vanity at its worst. From vanity to vanity, the race for power ultimately leads to the "vanity of vanities," the abyss.

The Vanity of Money

The same line of reasoning applies to money. Just as the hunger for power is never exhausted, so the love for wealth is never satisfied. Both of them, power and money, are vanity. Here also human effort leads to the void. The Hebrew phrase hammers the negation six times (5:7, 9, 11, 13, 14) to mark systematically that what starts as positive always ends as negative.

The first reason that wealth never satisfies is stated in the beginning as a subjective argument: The one who loves money will not be satisfied with money, and the one who loves abundance will not be satisfied with production (5:10). You will never get to the point where you will be satisfied, where you will finally realize the fruit.[5] The goal is never reached.

The second argument resorts to the objective observation that whatever you acquire will be taken and enjoyed by other people (5:11). The more you increase your wealth, the more there will be people to take advantage of it. You will not profit from it. You will just see it.

The third argument denies even the value of wealth, because it does not bring happiness. Ecclesiastes compares the sleep of the poor to the sleep of the rich (5:12). The quality of life of the poor person is better than that of the rich. Not only does the poor man sleep while the rich man cannot, his sleep also is "sweet." Apparently he has sweet dreams while the rich man is having nightmares and is pacing to and fro in his luxurious bedroom. The "sweet" quality of the poor man's sleep suggests that he is happier.

The fourth reason for the vanity of wealth is the most dramatic and also the most tangible argument. This last situation is worse than all the others (5:13–17). In this text, (1) the rich man did not see the increase of his wealth; (2) no one, not even his son, got the benefit of it; and (3) he didn't enjoy life. "All his days he also eats in darkness and he has much sorrow and sickness and anger" (5:17). All this labor and all the sacrifices were then "for the wind" (5:16).

Ecclesiastes imagines the scenario of someone who suddenly loses all his money, and he has nothing to leave to his newborn son (5:13, 14). Then right after the mention of the newborn, he makes this timely comment: "As he came from his mother's womb, naked shall he return, / To go as he came" (5:15). It is as if the formerly wealthy man was making that observation while looking at his own naked baby. Ecclesiastes uses the image of the newborn to convey the ultimate argument of death, in the terms of the Genesis curse: "Till you return to the ground, for out of it you were taken; for dust you are, and to dust you shall return" (Genesis 3:19). Furthermore, Ecclesiastes associates the curse with an allusion to the original nakedness of Adam and Eve, which belongs to the same context of the curse (Genesis 2:25; 3:7–12, 21). The curse of Genesis brings up the ultimate lesson of vanity: Why amass riches if we are destined to return to dust, where we cannot take anything with us (5:15)?

Ecclesiastes, however, is not against being wealthy and working hard and enjoying life. Rather, his argument concerns the eagerness to make money and accumulate wealth for the sake of wealth. He is also speaking against the fallacy that all this wealth can be achieved only through our own merits. His point is that all this human work is vanity, precisely because of the curse that puts on it the stamp of death. The only worthwhile and legitimate way of working and enjoying is within the context of the gift of God as the Creator.

In the concluding paragraph of the chapter (5:18–20), Ecclesiastes places us in that very perspective. The key words of the Creation story, "good" *(tov)* and "to give" *(natan),* both appear several times in our passage: "It is *good* . . . for one to eat and drink . . . and to enjoy the *good* of all his labor in which he toils under the sun all the days of his life which God *gives*. . . . As for every man to whom God has *given* riches and wealth, and given[6] him power to eat of it . . . and rejoice in his labor—this is the *gift* of God" (5:18, 19, emphasis supplied). Ecclesiastes insists that all this enjoyment, all this labor, and all this wealth are "good" precisely because they all are "the gift of God" in the context of Creation. This enjoyment is possible only because it is a received enjoyment, not because it is the result of our own work. Outside of this context, we are under the curse, in the realm of death and darkness, which Ecclesiastes calls *hebel,* "vanity."

---

1. See Lichtheim, vol. 1, 116.

2. The prayer *Kol Nidrey* ("all our vows") is recited at the beginning of the service of the Day of Atonement. It states that all kinds of vows made before God, unwittingly or rashly, during the year (and hence unfulfilled) shall be cancelled and declared null and void.

3. See Exodus 20:5, 6, where God's justice strikes to the "third and fourth generation", but His mercy is manifested to thousands of generations; compare Matthew 18:21–23. See also God's prayer in this Talmudic passage: "What is God's prayer? Rabbi Zutra says, 'may it be My will that My mercy overcome My anger, and My loving qualities override My strict traits, that I treat My children with My quality of mother's love and that I always deal with them beyond the letter of the law' " (Babylonian Talmud, *Berakhot* 7a).

4. See *Miqraot Gdoloth;* compare Ibn Ezra, "even the king, who has no superior, is subject to the field for its maintenance, for he subsists thereby."

5. The Hebrew word *tevuah,* translated "to increase" by NKJV, means "the product of the field" (see Leviticus 23:39; Joshua 5:12).

6. We do not count this word because in the Hebrew another word than *natan* is used.

CHAPTER 7

The Thirst of
the Soul

Even if we have everything, even if we accept it as the gift of God, we are still missing something essential. Ecclesiastes calls this lack a "great evil on man" (Ecclesiastes 6:1, translated literally). The New International Version refers to it as something that "weighs heavily on men." So far, the reasons we have given for vanity in life have been taken from this life itself: the lack of money, the lack of power, or simply the lack of life itself. The missing element has been within our reach. It may not always have been ours, but it was a part of this life. If it wasn't in our hands, at least it was either promised to us, it was in the other's hands, or it was available to us through hard work.

But Ecclesiastes made it clear that all these acquisitions were vanity, as long as they were not received as gifts from God. Now, taking the same track again, the author goes further, seeming though to contradict himself. He tells us that even if we receive all that we desire—great wealth, long life, and many children—and even if we get all of this as a legitimate and perfect blessing from God's hands by His grace, it is as if we have received nothing. It is still vanity (6:2, 3). He goes so far as to suggest that it would have been better for us that we did not receive anything at all (6:3). There is always something missing. Ecclesiastes deduces this from both poles of life—death and birth—and also deeper in the soul of every human being.

The Evidence of Death

The first argument is inspired from a firsthand experience. Ecclesiastes alludes to Solomon's career, referring to his "riches, wealth and honor" (6:2). This points directly to God's promise to Solomon: "I will give you riches and wealth and honor" (2 Chronicles 1:12). These are pure gifts God is giving to Solomon; Solomon did not even ask for them (2 Chronicles 1:11). The conclusion of the enjoyment of these goods is also hinted at in the parallel passage in 1 Kings 3:13: "I have also given you what you have not asked: both riches and honor . . . all your days." The use of the phrase "all your days" means "only during your life, and not beyond," an allusion to the loss of his kingdom, which was passed on to a foreigner, Jeroboam. Solomon received everything from God, "riches, wealth and honor," and did not lack anything of all he desired, just as Ecclesiastes described himself (2:10). It is clear, indeed, that Solomon is referring to himself in this passage, and his evaluation is negative: "This is vanity."

The lesson of this autobiography is that even God's gifts, as rich and fulfilling as they may be, remain vanity. We will die, and all that we acquired in wealth, wisdom, and honor will disappear or go to someone else. The reason for vanity is not the gift itself. Often, the gift survives the beneficiary. The gift could even be a perfect gift, coming from God. But what good is the gift if we are no longer there to enjoy it?

Nothing is more painful than dividing up the possessions of the dead. He is no longer here to wear the beautiful shirt he had worn so often. And, as we wear this shirt, we may feel the sense of vanity on our skin and remember the deceased. What we understand, then, is that it is not the vanity of the gift, but the vanity of the one who had enjoyed it and, paradoxically, our own vanity. The gift is in vain, simply because the one who receives it is in vain as well.

The point of Ecclesiastes is that what we miss has nothing to do with what we have. Rather, it has something to do with what we are, what will never be there, and what will always be missing. Ecclesiastes is not explicit; he simply notes the thirst.

The Evidence of Birth

The next argument is also taken from Solomon's experience, but this time Ecclesiastes alludes to his ambivalent experience with birth. The positive side of this ambivalent reference concerns the intensity of his life: "If a man begets a hundred children and lives many years" (6:3). Solomon was blessed with a long life, as promised by God (1 Kings 3:14) and, considering his many wives, he must have begotten many children, which is implied in the idea of "hundred" (Ecclesiastes 8:12).

The negative side relates to the death of David's first child with Bathsheba. It is significant that Solomon's birth is directly associated with that tragedy. Immediately after the announcement of the death of David's son, the Bible reports, "Then David comforted Bathsheba his wife, and went in to her and lay with her. So she bore a son, and he called his name Solomon" (2 Samuel 12:24). Solomon's birth, which holds the potential of many subsequent births, is connected to a false birth, the death of a newborn.

Solomon carries this tension in his argument and uses it to transform the blessing into a curse, and the curse into a blessing. Even if he "lives many years," still[1] "his soul is not satisfied" (6:3). The text may even suggest that he did not have a grave, implying the postponing of death.[2] His very long life, as full and fruitful as it was, had less value than the aborted child.[3] In a exaggerated manner, he balances the stillborn with the life of several thousand years: "Though it [the stillborn] has not seen the sun or known anything, this has more rest than that man, even if he lives a thousand years twice over" (6:5, 6). In the first argument, Ecclesiastes referred to death as the reason for vanity; now, he is saying that even without death (no grave, two thousand years of life), it is even worse. We are better off as a stillborn, having not existed at all.

What, then, is missing? What generates the sigh of Ecclesiastes? If it is neither the blessing of "riches, wealth, and honor," nor the blessing of a very long life, what is it? The question remains suspended in the void. Ecclesiastes just notices the gravity of the dissatisfaction.

The Evidence of Nostalgia

The first verse of the next paragraph sounds like a litany, reminding us of the song about Creation that prefaced Ecclesiastes' teaching. Notice the similarities: *"All [kol] the labor is for [le] his mouth, / And yet the soul is not satisfied [ml']"* (6:7, emphasis supplied), and *"All [kol] the rivers run into ['e] the sea, / Yet the sea is not full [ml']"* (1:7, emphasis supplied). The parallel between the two verses suggests the infinite character of the soul's dissatisfaction. Just as the

69

rivers run to the sea, and yet the sea is never full, so the labor goes to the mouth, and yet the mouth is never full.

Of course, this is a metaphor. The text does not refer to the glutton, who will never be satisfied, but to a more profound reality. By nature, men will never be satisfied. Whatever the quantity you bring into your mouth, it will never be satisfied—not because the mouth is too big, not because of an insatiable appetite, but because the need is never met. The thirst is always there.

The text repeats the phrase "the soul is not satisfied" (6:7; compare verse 3). The soul is not to be understood as a "spiritual" element, distinct from the body yet inside it, as purported by the Greek philosopher Plato and believed by many Christians and Jews since that time. The Hebrew word *nefesh* clearly implies the whole living being. In the Creation story, the soul *(nefesh)* is understood as the final result of the dynamic process of divine Creation, and not as a distinct element put inside the human body: "And the LORD God formed man of the dust of the ground, and breathed into his nostrils the breath of life; and man became a living being" (Genesis 2:7). The Hebrew word translated as *being* is *nefesh,* the word Ecclesiastes uses. What the Bible and Ecclesiastes understand as "soul" is nothing but the living person: ourselves.

It has been said that "man does not have a soul, he *is* a soul." The same Hebrew word *nefesh* is used in 6:2 and rendered by the word "himself." Every dimension of the human person is implied in that word; our passage clearly attests to this. The soul has spiritual as well as physical aspirations. The soul has "all he desires" (6:2). This includes physical desires, like longing for food (6:7) or something visible (6:9), but it also includes spiritual desires, such as longing for honor (6:2) or any "goodness" (6:3). It is noteworthy that all the parts of the human person are involved in that desire: the mouth (6:7), the eyes (6:9), the foot (6:8), and the human person (6:2). So when Ecclesiastes says that "the soul is not satisfied," he means that the whole human being is not satisfied. The need is not for more, but for something else, something that is not from here.

To express this longing of the soul, Ecclesiastes uses an idiomatic expression, "the wandering of desire [the soul]" (6:9), which suggests that the soul (our whole being) is figuratively going to another place. The Bible refers to the heart in a similar sense. When Elisha asks Gehazi, "Did not my heart go with you?" (2 Kings 5:26), he indicates the notion that his heart has gone elsewhere to the place where his thinking is. Likewise for Ecclesiastes, what is missing is not from here, from this life. Furthermore, this will always be missing; this need itself has an infinite quality. No one can provide for it. Even the wise man, although smarter than the fool, cannot do better than the fool on this matter (6:8). Even the theologian, who has access to the mysteries of God (at least he thinks he does), cannot know.

It is absurd, then, to try to multiply "words" [4] on this topic, for these many words will just "increase vanity" (6:11). If we remember that the Hebrew word for "vanity," *hebel,* means literally "vapor," we have here a living ironic metaphor: the more we speak about it, the more there is vapor . . . and nothing else. Theological discourses will not help; they will just add to the confusion.

What is missing belongs to another order. The wise and the fool have the same problem. They are both inhabited with the same infinite dissatisfaction. They both miss something they will never get. This thirst that is never quenched is for all men and women.

In the New Testament Jesus alludes to that thirst in his conversation with the Samaritan woman: " 'Whoever drinks of this water will thirst again, but whoever drinks of the water that I shall give him will never thirst' " (John 4:13, 14). In the book of Revelation, this thirst is mentioned again—humanity's thirst for God will finally be quenched: " 'To him who is thirsty I will give to drink without cost from the spring of the water of life' " (Revelation 21:6, NIV; compare 22:1). The image also appears in the context of *Sukkot,* the Feast of Tabernacles, when the Jews are in touch with the transitory character of life, the texture of vanity. On that occasion it was customary for the priest to draw water from the pool of Siloam with a golden jar during the morning and evening rituals of the daily sacrifices. The people greeted his return by singing, "With joy you will draw water from the wells of salvation" (Isaiah 12:3).[5] Here we touch upon a symptom shared by all mankind, that small depression which sometimes catches everyone, even the toughest of us. We are all visited by the same pinch of the heart, the same torturing thirst, which keeps reminding us that the essence of ourselves is not from here. The message of this passage resonates with the words of C. S. Lewis:

> Creatures are not born with desire unless satisfaction for those desires exists. A baby feels hunger: well, there is such a

thing as food. A duckling wants to swim: well, there is such a thing as water. Men feel sexual desire: well, there is such a thing as sex. If I find in myself a desire which no experience in this world can satisfy, the most probable explanation is that I was made for another world.[6]

In other words, this "desire, which no experience in this world can satisfy" is the very evidence, here in myself, of "another world."

The last line of chapter 6 suggests the same lesson through the image of the "shadow . . . under the sun" (6:12). Ecclesiastes compares the days of human life to the shadow. When Ecclesiastes asks the rhetorical question, "Who can tell what will be after it?" (see 6:12), that is, after the shadow,[7] he is then pointing to and affirming the existence of another reality—a hope, a nostalgia of the "good" of Creation that was lost.[8] In the same verse, Ecclesiastes himself refers to that "good," but he says that he is unable to grasp it in this life: "For who knows what is good for man in life?" (6:12). This rhetorical question, which implies a negative answer, is also a self-directed irony because several times Ecclesiastes offers an answer to that question. He is about to do it again in the next chapter.

---

1. This is an emphatic *waw* (see Bruce K. Waltke and Michael P. O'Connor, *An Introduction to Biblical Hebrew Syntax* [Winona Lake, Ind.: Eisenbrauns, 1990], 649).

2. Significantly, the only other passage that speaks about the absence of a grave is in relation to Moses' grave, thereby suggesting that he did not know death (Deuteronomy 34:6).

3. Although David's first child was not really a stillborn (he died only seven days after his birth), he was already declared dead even before his birth (2 Samuel 12:14); Ecclesiastes' hyperbolic style suggests that he may well have referred to him as a stillborn, in a similar way as Job speaks of the stillborn (Job 3:16; compare verse 11).

4. This translation of the Hebrew word *debarim* (instead of *things* by NKJV); see NIV: "The more the words, the less the meaning" (6:11).

5. Babylonian Talmud, *Taanith* 5a; *Tanhuma, Pekudei, 1.*

6. C. S. Lewis, *Mere Christianity* (New York: Simon and Schuster, 1996), 121.

7. The phrase translated "after him" by the NKJV could refer either to man or the shadow, or even to both of them, since man is the shadow (double entendre). The evocation of the sun in the expression "under the sun" may rather support the reference to the sun.

8. Paul refers to the same thing when he says "Now we see in a mirror, dimly, but then face to face. Now I know in part, but then I shall know just as I also am known" (1 Corinthians 13:12).

CHAPTER 8

Life Is Beautiful

We are reaching the second half of the book. The first section (chapters 1 through 6) was marked by the recurring refrain about vanity: This too is vanity and pursuit of wind (see Ecclesiastes 1:14; 2:11, 17, 26; 4:4, 16; 6:9). Most of the occurrences of the word *vanity* are found there.[1] The point of Ecclesiastes was the failure of the world, the vanity of life itself.

Ecclesiastes concluded that section with chapter 6, the shortest of the book, on the tragic note that even with all the "good" we could have received from God, we still had lost the original "good" *(tov):* "Who knows what is good for man in life?" (6:12). Ecclesiastes implied that no one knew what was good. He did not just mean that humans lacked information; in Hebrew thought, "knowing" is a dynamic and existential experience. Not knowing good means, then, that we are unable to experience what is good; we are unable to *be* good.

It is remarkable that the same association of the two words "to know" and "good" is used in Genesis 2 and 3 in relation to the tree of knowledge of good and evil. The passage, however, that resonates the most with this phrase of Ecclesiastes is Genesis 3:22 because, as does this verse of Ecclesiastes, it is the only passage that relates the knowledge of good with man and life: "And the LORD God said, Behold, the man is become [was] as one of us, to know good and evil: and now, lest he put forth his hand, and take also of the tree of life, and eat, and live for ever" (KJV). The two biblical passages share four words in common; in fact all the words of Ecclesiastes' question are present in the Genesis verse: "to know," "good," "man" (Adam), and "life." This strong echo suggests that Ecclesiastes is alluding here to Genesis 3:22.

To understand what Ecclesiastes means, we need, then, to understand the Genesis verse. In this text, God is saying that before he took the fruit, man "was," or "had been,"[2] like God concerning knowledge of good and evil. As long as man did not disobey God, he "knew." Paradoxically, only if we are in the good are we able to discern between good and evil. As soon as Adam and Eve sinned, they left the good and consequently lost the discernment which Genesis calls "the knowledge between good and evil." From then on, evil and good were confused. Evil was mingled with good, and good mingled with evil.

Ellen White's comments on this tragic incident are to the point: "Man lost all because he chose to listen to the deceiver rather than to Him who is Truth, who alone has understanding. By the mingling of evil with good, his mind had become confused, his mental and spiritual powers benumbed. No longer could he appreciate the good that God had so freely bestowed."[3]

This is the confusion of mind Ecclesiastes is reflecting on. Man lost the knowledge of the good. He could not "appreciate the good" anymore, and therefore mixed up good and evil, and wisdom fled from him. Yet Ecclesiastes does not despair, nor does he keep us in the chaos of vanity and in the dream of the good. Oddly enough, from the lucid observation of the loss of the good, he moves to life, attempting to cope with the ambiguity of good and evil, and the elusiveness of wisdom.

The Ambiguity of Good and Evil

Ecclesiastes just concluded that no one knows what is good (tov). Yet in the next section, the word tov "good" (usually translated "better"), is repeated nine times. Now the good is balanced with its opposite; we discover it in unexpected places where we would normally find the opposite. But this is the logical implication of the ambiguous character of "good."

It starts with a play on words, which works best if you can hear it in Hebrew: "shem tov mishemen tov." In English: "A good name is better than a precious ointment." This expression is placed in parallel to the phrase, "And the day of death than the day of one's birth" (7:1). In order to prove that death (the negative) is better than birth (the positive), Ecclesiastes relates death and birth respectively to the name and the perfume (ointment).

In the ancient Near East, a name was very important. It stood for the person and meant his reputation. The Bible tells us that "David made himself a name when he returned from killing eighteen thousand Syrians" (2 Samuel 8:13). Even God is said to have "made a name" for Himself at the time of the Exodus (Nehemiah 9:10). But the name was also associated with death and immortality. The name of the wicked died with them (Proverbs 10:7), while the name of the righteous (or in ancient Egypt, the name of the scribes, or the wise men) achieved immortality.[4]

No one would contest the ringing accuracy of this proverb. If the name and the good memory, which are just abstractions in one's mind, are better than the tangible precious perfume, then the day of death is better than the day of birth. Using irony, Ecclesiastes makes his point: death, like a good name, is valuable; life, like perfume, is vanity.

However, Ecclesiastes is not saying that death per se has more value than life per se. His point is that death helps you put life in the right perspective, making life less vain and more meaningful. No wonder, then, that Ecclesiastes finds the wise man in the house of mourning and the fool in the house of feasting (7:2). Being exposed to death, whether during a funeral, in a war, or because of a threatening disease, you may change your life. Death obliges you to be genuine, to live your real self, to cast away that false plastic image that you have spent years perfecting. Death teaches you to think beyond the present moment; it trains you to orient your life to the future.

A real brush with death also makes life more precious. Your taste of life is no longer the same. You do not take life for granted any more. You breathe differently. You eat differently. You love differently. You see people differently. Life is changed: You are more alive.

Life takes another turn in the feasting houses—pubs, clubs, restaurants, cinemas, casinos, malls, and theme parks. Sure, these places help you to forget; you can forget your pain and anguish. But these places also force you to forget who you are. These places have all the necessary equipment to entertain you and steal you from yourself. They make you drink. They make you try exciting new things. They kill your sense of time and distract you. They make you laugh and feel good. They give you the perfect illusion that you are enjoying life, when in fact you will come out of these houses the shadow of yourself—sick, sad, more anguished than ever. You will lose the taste for life. You will ultimately drag yourself to death.

Thus the paradoxical principle of Ecclesiastes is verified: The places of joy and amusement actually contain the germs of death. And the houses of mourning and sadness turn out to carry the promise of life.

But Ecclesiastes is not suggesting that regular attendance at houses of mourning will be enough to make us genuinely wise. Funeral parlor directors are not necessarily wiser than other professionals. Ecclesiastes is simply urging us, in concrete terms, to think about death, so that we realize the vanity of life. And as we contemplate the vanity of our own life, we will subsequently be reoriented to the true face of life. We will reconnect with the essence of ourselves, the "good" hidden in the deep folds of our souls. Then we will belong to another world, what the New Testament called the kingdom of God. Ironically, by making us confront the reality of death, Ecclesiastes takes us to the other reality. Obviously, the houses of amusement do the opposite. They distract us from death, and by doing so they keep us away from that other landscape.

Ecclesiastes applies the same lesson to other situations. The rebuke of the wise will have the same effect. It will make us face ourselves. It will disturb us and shake the comfort of our mediocrity, the illusion that we are doing well. It will oblige us to move from the easy to the difficult, from the familiar to the unknown. The mechanism of this experience is the same as the experience of death. By saying no to us, by pushing us down, by crushing us, the rebuke will force us to come out of ourselves and put us in touch with what is above. As teachers and parents understand very well, this is the way education functions. Rebuke and correction are prerequisites for learning, the only way to discover something else and do better.

On the opposite side, we hear the song of the fools. This song, unlike the rebuke of the wise, has a melody that is pleasant to the ears and the soul. We love it. Unlike the wise, who stands alone, the fools are many; they are therefore more alluring and convincing. This is the popular voice. Unlike the single rebuke[5] of the wise, fools are noisy and cracking jokes. Ecclesiastes compares their laughter to "the crackling of thorns under the pot." Not a very intelligent laughter, not very meaningful; like thorns in the fire, they generate more noise than heat. The laughter sounds like a cascade; it is contagious and is echoed by others. The fools are laughing at the wise, and the noise of their jokes covers the sensible words of the wise. Ultimately, the mockery will turn into an unbearable oppressing derision (7:7).

In Hebrew, we hear a pun that connects the laughter *(sehoq)* and the pressure *('osheq),* suggesting that the peer pressure, which may even include bribes (7:7), will ultimately affect the wise and turn him into a fool.

It is not easy to remain faithful when you feel ridiculous and different. Again, we hear the same paradoxical message. It is in the difficult resistance, in the discomfort of the minority, that we will reach the "good" and survive vanity, rather than in the fun and beautiful life. Yet Ecclesiastes warns us that risks await the candidates of wisdom and righteousness. The majority will inevitably single us out and make martyrs of us.

First is the risk of impatience. It is one thing to commit ourselves to the right cause, to make the courageous decision to walk alone in the crowd of the scoffers; it is another thing to stay there. The brave doctor of Camus' novel *The Plague* reminds us that "it is easier to be a hero than a saint." It is easier to die for God than to live for Him. Dying takes only a moment; living takes years. Also, there is more exaltation and glory in being a martyr than in patiently, daily, resisting both open and subtle assaults from outside and the impulses from inside. "The patient in spirit is better than the proud in spirit" (7:8). This is why "the end of a thing is better than its beginning" (7:8), because the zealous runner at the beginning of a race often is absent at the finish line. To follow Ecclesiastes' metaphor, the crackling thorns are quick to be engulfed in flame, and they are very vocal about it, but their fire does not last long. Only the end will testify to the quality of our commitment.

Ironically, there is a great risk of pride derived from the fact that we have the wisdom and the truth that the world's many "fools" don't have. The Hebrew word translated as "proud" implies the idea of height; we see ourselves higher than others and despise them and are even angry with them because they do not understand. Jesus' disciples were so convinced about the truth that they wanted to call down fire from heaven to consume the Samaritan who didn't believe (Luke 9:54).

Note that Ecclesiastes does not question the wisdom and the truth that we claim to have over others. Solomon does not deny the reality of truth and of wisdom; in fact, he recognizes the superiority of wisdom and knowledge over error and ignorance (7:12; compare 2:13). Neither does he play the card of pluralism. He does not say that everyone is right and that truth is everywhere. What bothers Ecclesiastes is when truth and wisdom become haughtiness and self-righteousness, or when truth becomes the reason for anger (7:9). He is troubled when truth and wisdom ultimately degenerate into fanaticism and extremism, when the conviction to be right leads to finger pointing, and when the duty to rebuke leads to child abuse. It disturbs Ecclesiastes when our arrogance reaches the point where, like Elijah, we say, "I alone am left" (1 Kings 19:10), failing to even acknowledge our debt to the heritage of the past. Ecclesiastes repeatedly responded to this claim, reminding us that the wisdom we claim to have found has already been proclaimed (1:10; 6:10).

Now he takes it a step further and challenges those who question the value of the past: " 'Why were the former days better than these?' " (7:10). Ecclesiastes emphasizes the importance of the past, of its heritage and lessons. Though we may be tempted to despise those who came before us because "they were wrong" or outdated, what we have received from them is as important as our own findings. "Wisdom is as good as heritage," (7:11, author's translation)[6] says Ecclesiastes. The problem that concerns Ecclesiastes is the ambiguity of good, the troubling fact that shadows of vanity—arrogance, pride, and impatience, along with fanaticism and extremism—have found their way even into the light of wisdom.

The imperative "see!" is used twice, first when Ecclesiastes urges us to "consider the work of God," (7:13) and second when he invites us to "consider in the day of adversity" (7:14). We have to approach adversity the same way as we approach the work of God. The reason for this advice is immediately given. God "made" both, just as He created the world. Ecclesiastes uses 'asah, "made,", the word that describes God's work of creation. The God of Creation stands behind both.

The lesson Ecclesiastes draws from this observation is that we should learn to welcome both, "the one as well as the other" (7:14), literally "this besides this," the good and the bad, because we do not know what comes after it (referring to the bad).[7] We do not know the future of the bad event. But since God is in control, we can only hope.

Ecclesiastes is not promoting a masochist ideal; he is not suggesting that we should enjoy the bad. The verb "enjoy" is used for the good; but for the bad, he uses the word "see." It is the same verb as when we see with our own eyes the visible creation, implying the same attitude of awe, question, and reflection. This is the "see" of the lucidity that does not deny the reality of evil, which faces it; but it is also the "see" of the attention that pauses and waits for what comes after, which we cannot anticipate.

Thus the wise man is called to live in tension. On one hand, he will fully enjoy the present good; on the other hand, he will see the bad and learn to "wait and see," simultaneously accepting both of them.

The Ambiguity of Ethics

The author then applies the training of living in tension to the intricacies of ethical life. The fact that you are righteous and devote yourself to the good does not prevent you from "perishing," which is normally the fate of the wicked.[8] Conversely, the wicked man may well live a long life, which is normally the reward of the righteous (7:15).

Ecclesiastes' intention here is not to challenge traditional wisdom,[9] as he already did in another context (3:16).[10] His point is that the bad may be found within the act of righteousness and, conversely, the good may be found within the act of wickedness.

Ecclesiastes shows this ambiguity of good and evil in the perfectionist mania. The "too good" is bad, and the "too bad" is also bad. Just as the fanatic for God and for the truth can be dangerous and can turn his original wisdom into foolishness (7:9), so the perfectionist can create hell on earth. So eager to do exactly the very right thing, he will not only become an unbearable pain for his neighbors but in the process destroy himself (7:16). The same principle applies to the "overly wicked"; he will also die because of his excesses (7:17). To add bad to the already bad will make it worse.

Ecclesiastes' ethical advice, then, is consistent with that ambiguity: "It is good that you grasp this, and also not remove your hand from the other" (7:18). It is clear that he is referring to the good and to the bad. The expression "this" *(zeh),* used twice, referring to both the good and the bad in verse 14, reappears here. Is Ecclesiastes encouraging ethical decisions based on compromise, a middle way between good and evil? Is he suggesting some kind of mixture of good and evil? Certainly not! What Ecclesiastes is saying is that good and evil are, indeed, already mixed up. Truth is not black and white. Good is ambiguous, just as bad is. This is Ecclesiastes' problem. This is our problem, too, ever since the Fall.

For Ecclesiastes, the only way to survive this dilemma is the fear of God: "For he who fears God will escape them all" (7:18). In using the word *all,* Ecclesiastes refers to the tension that encompasses the two opposites, good and bad.[11] The only way, then, to break through the problem of confusion between good and evil is to have wisdom from above: "Wisdom strengthens the wise" (7:19). This wisdom must come from above, because "there is not a just man on earth who does good / And does not sin" (7:20). Man by himself cannot make it. Our only help is the wisdom from God, the One who is completely "good" and has never compromised with evil.

As far as humans are concerned, we are all sinners. This applies to you, says Ecclesiastes, as well as to the other: "Also do not take to heart everything people say, / Lest you hear your servant cursing you" (7:21). This admonition is a direct application of the principle we just discussed in verse 20. No one is exempt from sin. The issue of hearing someone cursing us or simply discrediting us[12] is secondary. Ecclesiastes is using that illustration to urge us to be as tolerant toward the other as we are toward ourselves.

Ecclesiastes chooses this last sin because it affects our relationship to the other and has a significant impact on our whole behavior: "We all stumble in many things. If anyone does not stumble in word, he is a perfect man, able also to bridle the whole body" (James 3:2). It is indeed easy to recognize that we are not perfect and to forgive ourselves for our own mistakes; it is not as easy to recognize that the others are not perfect and to forgive them for theirs. The awareness that I am not perfect should help me to be tolerant and forgiving of others' imperfection: "For many times, also, your heart has known / That even you have cursed others" (7:22). Because we are all sinners, our help and our salvation could come only from the outside. Only the wisdom from God, who never sinned, will help us sort out the confusion between good and evil.

Elusive Wisdom

Considering the ambiguous nature of good and evil, wisdom will not be found easily. Significantly, from 10:24 to 10:29, the key word "to find" occurs seven times. Ecclesiastes tells the story of his frustration and failure in that hide-and-seek adventure: "I said, 'I will be wise' " (7:23). The Hebrew form of the verb indicates his good will, his determination: I said [within myself]: I strongly want to be wise.[13] Yet he stumbles on two obstacles.

The first obstacle has to do with the wisdom itself. Wisdom is "far" and "deep." These words are often associated with God Himself: God's judgments are far (Psalm 10:5), God Himself is far (Psalm 22:1, 19; Proverbs 15:29). God is also described as the one who "uncovers deep things out of darkness" (Job 12:22), who "reveals deep and secret things" (Daniel 2:22). Saying that wisdom is "far" and "deep" is to suggest that it pertains to God and that humans have no access to it except through divine revelation.

Ecclesiastes is then implying that his effort is vain. His rhetorical question, "Who can find it out?" (7:24), with its implied negative answer, confirms the impossibility of the task. The imagery and language he is using to characterize wisdom are also significant. Wisdom is personified as a woman, and his research takes on the form of a love affair. The motif of seeking and not finding borrows the language from a lover's pursuit.[14] Here, the elusive lover is Wisdom herself. Ecclesiastes has pursued her but has never been able to find her. In fact our text alludes to the ideal woman of Proverbs 31, who is the very embodiment of Wisdom herself. Here Ecclesiastes uses the same words as in Proverbs 31:10, "Who can find it out . . . far." Clearly, Ecclesiastes wants to emphasize that humans cannot attain wisdom. They can only search and ask for it. But they will never be satisfied.

The second obstacle to attaining wisdom has to do with the mess caused by the apparent ambiguity of wisdom, which is associated with folly. Ecclesiastes' seeking for wisdom is associated with his seeking for folly:

"I applied my heart to know,
To search and seek out wisdom . . .
To know the wickedness of folly,
Even of foolishness and madness" (7:25).

The Hebrew verb that introduces the process of searching, *sbb,* "turn around" (translated here as "I applied"), is the same as in 1:6, where it applied to the endless circling of the wind. Here, it suggests the endless back and forth movements of his search.

Ecclesiastes' difficult task is now to sort out the positive and the negative. The Hebrew word that describes this operation, *heshbon,* is a commercial term well known in the ancient Near East; it means "accounting" or "balance."[15] Ecclesiastes' attempt to know the negative—wickedness, folly, foolishness, and madness—is accompanied by his positive search for "wisdom and accounting" (7:25, author's translation). Like a merchant or an accountant going over a commercial document, Ecclesiastes tries to sort out where each item belongs. In traditional thinking, wisdom and foolishness are clearly distinct from each other. This is not the case for Ecclesiastes. It is as if the accountant is confused and is unable to find a clear distinction between wisdom/righteousness and folly/wickedness. A paraphrase of the Hebrew phrase shows Ecclesiastes' embarrassment in placing wickedness and folly—"to know the wicked side of folly and the foolish side of madness" (7:25, author's translation). This confusion is reflected in the imagery of "the woman" (7:26). Folly is represented by a woman, just as wisdom was. When Ecclesiastes is complaining about the threat of that woman ("I find more bitter than death / The woman"), he is not speaking against women in general or in particular. "The woman" (with the definite article) he has in mind is "the folly," the only noun in the preceding verse that has a definite article. This Woman Folly, then, is set over the Woman Wisdom, much like the two women in Proverbs 9. There Woman Wisdom, representing life and righteousness (Proverbs 9:1–12), is opposed to Woman Folly, representing death and wickedness (Proverbs 9:13–18).[16]

In introducing a new (third) paragraph (7:27–29), Ecclesiastes again plays the accountant, trying to draw up the balance: "Adding one thing to the other to find out the reason" (literally, "one to one to find the balance," 7:27). The word *heshbon,* "accounting" or "balance," is used, just as in 7:25. Ecclesiastes describes himself struggling to sort out the positive and the negative. His concern is "to find." Most of the occurrences of the word "to find" are concentrated in this paragraph (five out of the seven). The word "still" indicates that this search is not new, "which my soul still seeks, but I cannot find" (7:28). Again it is the same elusive woman he was trying to find in the first paragraph (7:23, 24).

Ecclesiastes' remark "a woman . . . I have not found" (7:28) should not be understood as an expression of his misogynistic bias; he is simply talking again about the wisdom that always eludes him. The contrast between the woman he cannot find and the man he can find is intended to emphasize the elusiveness of that woman. "I can find a human *('adam)* who would be better than a thousand, but a woman, in all these, I cannot find" (7:28, author's translation). As this literal translation indicates, he is not talking about the superiority of men over women. The fact that he uses the word *'adam,* "human," shows that he has in mind humanity and not a specific male in contrast to a woman. It is also significant that the word *'adam* is used in the next verse (7:29) where it clearly refers to humanity, since the pronoun that follows is the plural "they." In fact, in forty-eight other instances in the book, this usage always refers to humans in general and never to a male. When a specific male is intended, the word *'ish* is used (see Ecclesiastes 6:2 and 9:14, 15). If Ecclesiastes meant to contrast the human male to the human female, he would have used *'ish,* not *'adam.*[17]

Ecclesiastes says that it is possible to find one human better than a thousand, implying the rarity of that human being, but as far as a woman is concerned, the Woman Wisdom that is, it is impossible (not just rare) to find her among all the humans. He is insisting on this point over and over again: Wisdom will always stay beyond the human reach. The reason, as he already pointed out in verse 20, is human nature. Presently, humans are reduced to the task of the accountant, trying to sort out the good from the bad, trying to cope with the ambiguity of good and evil. This is the only thing that is reserved to us.

Ecclesiastes concludes his chapter with this acknowledgment: "Truly, this only I have found; that God made man *('adam)* upright, but [now], they are reduced to much accounting" (7:29, author's translation). Ecclesiastes uses again the word *heshbon* ("accounting" or "balance"), and the phrase is the same as in 7:25; therefore it should mean the same thing. Ecclesiastes reminds us that, originally, man was created "upright." He was totally in the "good." But, since the fall, good got mixed with the bad, and man is now struggling to sort out one from the other, trying to distinguish between wisdom and foolishness—and (we might add) not with much success, either.

---

1. Twenty-four occurrences out of the thirty-eight in the whole book.

2. The Hebrew word is *hayah*, in the perfect form, implying a past tense, just as in "now the serpent was *[hayah]* more cunning" (Genesis 3:1). The verb should then not be translated by "has become," implying the theological aberration that man became like God only when he sinned, which would then confirm what the serpent was saying (Genesis 3:5).

3. Ellen G. White, *Education* (Mountain View, Calif.: Pacific Press®, 1952), 25.

4. Lichtheim, vol 1, 181; vol. 2, 175–177.

5. The word is normally in plural in the Bible. This is the only occurrence where the word is in the singular, suggesting an intentional usage.

6. The preposition *'im* (often translated "with") has also the meaning "as," like in 2:16; see James L. Crenshaw, *Ecclesiastes: A Commentary,* The Old Testament Library (Philadelphia, Pa.: Westminster Press, 1987), 138.

7. The "day of adversity," as the last antecedent, qualifies better than "man," which is its immediate subject.

8. The Hebrew verb *'abad* ("to perish") always applies to the wicked in Wisdom literature (see Proverbs 10:28; 11:7, 10; 28:28, etc.).

9. See Deuteronomy 4:26, 40; 5:16; 11:9; Proverbs 28:16; etc.

10. Compare Job 12:17; 21:13; Psalm 73:2, 3.

11. The same usage of *all* is attested in 2:14, where it refers to the two opposites wise and fool and in 3:19, where it refers to the two opposites men and beasts.

12. The Hebrew word *qelala,* usually translated "curse," may also mean "to slight," "to discredit" (see Leviticus 19:14; Judges 9:27; Jeremiah 24:9; 49:13, etc.); it has that meaning in 10:20, when we are urged not to speak or think badly about the king or the rich.

13. It is a cohortative form that expresses "the direction to an action and denotes especially self-encouragement" (E. Kautzsch, ed., *Gesenius' Hebrew Grammar,* 2d English ed. [Oxford: The Clarendon Press, 1910], § 48e).

14. See especially Song of Songs 3:1–6; 5:6; Proverbs 1:28; 18:22.

15. The word is translated by NKJV as "reason of things."

16. The same imagery reappears in the book of Revelation; for the good woman, see Revelation 12:1–6, 13–17, and for the bad woman, see Revelation 17:1–18.

17. Compare, for instance, Genesis 2:23, 24.

Crime and Punishment

We just learned about man's struggle trying to catch wisdom. And now, "wisdom makes his face shine" (Ecclesiastes 8:1), as if he has finally caught the elusive woman. The phrase sounds familiar, like the priestly blessing. As part of the temple cult, this blessing was extended every morning and evening at the daily offering. The priests standing on a special platform, the *doukhan,* pronounced this blessing:

The LORD bless you and keep you;
The LORD make His face shine upon you,
And be gracious to you;
The LORD lift up His countenance upon you,
And give you peace (Numbers 6:24–26).

In the memory of Israel, then, the phrase "makes His face shine" is associated with the blessing of God and the subsequent promise of grace and peace. With this reminiscence, Ecclesiastes means that wisdom will make the wise person's face shine; by implication, the wise man is expected to be gracious and peaceful toward others.

Ecclesiastes adds that the "sternness of his face is changed." The Hebrew word *'oz'* for "sternness" has the connotation of "arrogance" or "impudence."[1] This is always the temptation of the wise, that is, to become arrogant and disrespectful.

"Who is like the wise?" (8:1, NIV) Ecclesiastes asks with irony. The man who is respectful to others, who looks upon them with favor and grace, and who remains humble toward them—he is "like the wise." The wise is the man who knows his limits and is (paradoxically) aware of his lack of wisdom. The wise man is the one who pursues wisdom, not the one who catches it. The experience of this elusive wisdom is now illustrated in real life, in facing the power of the king and the unfairness of life.

God Save the King

It is in our best interest to respect authorities. Ecclesiastes founds his counsel on a religious basis. His language is typically religious. In order to refer to the king's order, he uses the Hebrew word *mitswah,* "commandment," the word normally used for God's commandments. The whole phrase "Who may say to him, 'what are you doing?' " (8:4) is the exact replica of Job 9:12 (compare Daniel 4:35), where it refers to God. He also specifies, "for the sake of your oath to God" (8:2). The expression "oath to God" (or literally, "oath of God") is usually associated with some kind of sacred covenant between two parties.[2]

The text seems to allude more specifically to one particular incident, which was precisely marked by this oath and that involved Solomon himself. The king had made a covenant under that "oath of God" between himself and Shimei, a member of Saul's family (1 Kings 2:43, 44). This text shares with our passage (8:2–5) a significant number of common words and associations: "oath of God," "keep commandment," and "evil/wickedness" *('ra)*. What is interesting about Shimei is that he was already well known for his lack of respect to King David; he cursed him and threw stones at him but was spared at that time (2 Samuel 16:5–13; compare 2 Samuel 19:18–23).

Ecclesiastes is not just seeking a way to support his own kingly authority by appealing to the divinely commanded duty to respect the king. David refrained from touching Saul because he was "the anointed of the Lord" (1 Samuel 24:6, compare 26:11). This religious reference in regard to our attitude toward authorities may seem odd, with the still-fresh memory of fascist and authoritarian regimes. Yet the principle remains valid, inasmuch as it teaches us about the reality of life: As Ecclesiastes already warned, there will always be someone above you (Ecclesiastes 5:8).

Beyond this practical advice, however, and in order to learn to cope with that unavoidable reality, the religious connection contains a valuable piece of education. In learning to respect authority, whether in the family, the government, or at the police station, we develop a sense of awe and of transcendence. This, in turn, prepares us to apprehend another reality, one that surpasses us and draws us closer to the infinite and mysterious presence of God. It is because we have lost the sense of that transcendence that we have lost the sense of respecting each other. As Abraham Heschel said, We have lost the sense of brotherhood because we have lost the sense of fatherhood.[3] In working to develop within our soul the sense of transcendence, we will learn to see the other beyond ourselves and accept his/her differences. We will create more solid families. We will promote a more civil society, with greater respect for the old and the weak, and more respect for laws, even those that do not immediately seem relevant. We will save our society from its present chaos.

But some will not be convinced by such a "spiritual" reason. Therefore, Ecclesiastes adds a more visible, more pressing reason: the fear of punishment and the reward of security. Listen to his words: "Do not take your stand for an evil thing, for he does whatever pleases him" (8:3), and "He who keeps his command will experience nothing harmful" (8:5). The story of Shimei perfectly illustrates this lesson. As long as he respected the king, he could argue on his own behalf and save himself (2 Samuel 19:20). But as soon as he failed to his commitment to the king, he paid dearly for his "wickedness" (1 Kings 2:44); Solomon had him executed (1 Kings 2:46). This principle of just retribution, already in this life, is repeated over and over again in the Bible, emerging particularly in the context of Wisdom tradition (Proverbs 19:16).

Life, therefore, is not as simple and clear as suggested by this principle and by the experience of Shimei. It often happens that the king abuses his power. Even the above example shows an abuse of power on the part of Solomon. David, his father, had forgiven Shimei for a much worse fault. Having Shimei killed simply because he failed in his promise not to go to Jerusalem is a disproportionate punishment. Ecclesiastes does not exclude, then, the scenario of an unjust treatment. He knows by experience that abuses of power and oppression are being perpetrated under the king, and often by the king himself. It often happens that innocents are put into jail and tortured for nothing. The principle of just retribution does not work for them in this life, and the oppressor remains unpunished.

But for Ecclesiastes there is still justice and a time for it. He calls this "time and judgment" [4] (8:5). Ecclesiastes already used these two words together to refer to the same event. In conjunction to the same situation of injustice and human impotence to deal with it, he says that "God shall judge" and "there shall be a time there for every purpose and for every work" (3:17). God will render judgment in God's time. The wise man knows that (8:5). Though the wise man has no control over time and the process of the judgment (8:7), he knows that the event will take place. That is all he knows. Judgment per se, like wisdom, is in God's hands alone.

Meanwhile, in the course of our earthly existence, we have to content ourselves with the idea that one day even the powerful superior will die. He will then be unable to "retain the air" *(ruach)* within himself (8:8, author's translation). With all the power he has, he has no power over "the day of death" (8:8); for "the day of death," just as the "day of birth," is not in his control (see 3:2; 7:1). We do not choose the day of our death, as we do not choose the day of our birth. With all the means the powerful person has at his disposal, he cannot even have himself exempted or replaced (8:8). Death is the great equalizer. In death we are all the same—the wise and the fool (2:16), humans and animals (3:19, 20), and now, the king and the humble subject.

However, a slight nuance has been introduced in our passage. Until here, Ecclesiastes used this argument to show the vanity of our life. But now, he speaks of the death of the oppressor. Even Hitler's SS forces, even the brutal and sadistic torturer, even the violent terrorist who plays God and decides the death of others, will die. This death challenges their claim for superiority; from the point of view of the victim, it means some kind of judgment reestablishing the balance that had been upset. The victim feels vindicated.

Ecclesiastes even suggests that a judgment is already at work here. He has observed that crime has also an effect on the perpetrator— "One man rules over another to his own hurt" (8:9). Human nature is such that abuses do not just harm the abused. The oppressor is deeply affected, socially and psychologically. An oppressor does not have any friends. He always lives in suspicion. He is never in peace with himself or with the others. As the prophet Isaiah says, "There is no peace . . . for the wicked" (Isaiah 48:22). Mysteriously, the harm we inflict on others ultimately reaches us, in the depth of our soul and in the mechanism of our mental balance. The recent works of psychosomatic medicine have indeed revealed the reality of that profound connection.

Ecclesiastes' observation, then, confirms the traditional view of retribution as expressed in many places in the Bible, particularly in Deuteronomy and Job. The wicked man is cursed and therefore receives his punishment already within his earthly existence, while the righteous man is blessed and his good actions are rewarded. The wicked man is unhappy and will live a short and poor life, while the righteous man is happy and will live a long and rich life (Proverbs 2:21, 22; 10:27). Yet, we know, and Ecclesiastes knows as well, that this theory does not really work. In fact it happens often the other way around.

When Good Things Happen to Bad People and Bad Things Happen to Good People

From the court of the king, Ecclesiastes moves to the streets of life. He sees there what he had already observed, even with the king—injustice. Evil is flourishing: "The heart of the sons of men is fully set in them to do evil" (8:11). In the present, the wicked man is successful. "A sinner does evil a hundred times" (8:12). Not just once. He keeps doing evil, repeatedly, and nothing gets in his way. Judgment does not strike him. On the contrary, he lives a long life; "his days are prolonged" (8:12). And then, when he dies, he receives all the funeral honors in the "place of holiness" (8:10). Even in the religious place he is recognized. He appears to be blessed.

Ecclesiastes does not understand. What "occurs on earth" (8:14) has shaken his whole logical system of justice: "There are just men to whom it happens according to the work of the wicked; again, there are wicked men to whom it happens according to the work of the righteous" (8:14). Ecclesiastes has the courage and the lucidity to face the problem. He sees that the righteous suffer, and that the wicked succeed. He also knows that this situation is not normal, considering God's presence. He is confronted with two alternatives. He can either take the position of Job's friends: The fact that he suffers shows that he is not righteous; or he can take the position of the skeptic: The fact that there is no judgment shows that there is no God. Ecclesiastes chooses neither option.

Ecclesiastes stands on the side of the victims—against Job's friends, against the "good" religious people of all ages, against the professional defenders of God. Suffering does not necessarily mean God's punishment, and happiness does not necessarily mean God's blessing.

The fact that a man gets sick does not mean that he did not eat correctly. We know many people who faithfully observe all dietary principles, exercise regularly, and live a healthy life, and yet they get sick and die. The fact that a woman has AIDS does not mean she has committed adultery. She could have been born with the virus or she could have contracted it through a blood transfusion. The fact that a girl was raped does not mean she acted wrongly. Poverty is not always the product of laziness and mismanagement. Unpredictable accidents, a storm, or simply the lack of vital resources in the land may cause suffering. Or sometimes even the decision to tell the truth, to remain faithful to ethical or religious principles, may play a determining role in poverty. We could prolong the list forever. Starving little babies of Africa with their swollen bellies, Jews gassed at Auschwitz, and Rwandans massacred—all are the most dramatic demonstration of that observation. It would be monstrous to try to make sense of these tragedies and refuse to see the unjust side of it.

At the same time, happiness and success do not necessarily mean God's approval and blessing. The fact that someone is in good health and lives long does not mean that he is righteous. The pimp who exploits young girls and enjoys a good life on the Riviera; the mediocre employee who uses flattery and lies in order to reach higher positions; the former SS officer who fled to South America and prospered there, founded a happy family, and died at an old age. All these examples of success and happiness confirm Ecclesiastes' observation. To try to find God's support there would be sacrilegious, for it would involve Him in those iniquities.

Against the skeptic with whom he shares the same recognition of injustice, Ecclesiastes insists that there is a God and that, in spite of all, it is better to live with Him: "I surely know that it will be well with those who fear God, who fear before Him. But it will not be well with the wicked" (8:12, 13). It is interesting that Ecclesiastes uses the technical Hebrew word *tov,* "good," (translated here as "well"), key word of the Creation story, to describe the advantage of living with God. The one who fears God is in touch with the original state of Creation. He comes to live with the perspective of the original plan, and not the one that has been distorted by the accident of evil and death. He is able to see beyond the present condition; he has the memory of what things were initially and what they should be. He is visited by the future. His life has a future direction. At the same time, it is interesting that the verb *to fear,* associated with fearing God, is used in the future tense. He lives, acts, and has perspective.

On the contrary, the one who does not fear God, whom Ecclesiastes calls "the wicked" (8:13), has no perspective. He is just in the present. The verbs associated with him are in the present tense. His heart "is being full" (8:11, author's translation), he is depicted as "sinning," "doing" evil (8:12), "not fearing" (8:13). He is just there like a dead thing, with no initiative of his own, without any future orientation.

It is also significant that the verb *to prolong,* applied to the life of the wicked, is used in the present (8:12); it applies only to the present existence. But when the same verb is used in the future tense, it comes with a negation: "nor will he prolong his days" (8:13). This change of tense suggests that the wicked may well enjoy a long life on earth, and thus prolong his iniquity, as the ambiguity of expression may imply. But this enjoyment is limited to the present, futureless life, a life whose ephemeral character is compared to the shadow (8:13). The wicked will not enjoy a life with a future. Ecclesiastes alludes here to another order, where there is a future.

The Ambiguity of Joy

For Ecclesiastes, happiness is ambiguous. It is a bittersweet experience. On one side he "praises" joy: "I commended enjoyment" (8:15). The Hebrew word for *praise* "I commended," is a technical word for praising God (Psalms 145:4; 147:12). Happiness is enjoyed as we enjoy God Himself. Humans are urged to receive the gift the Creator has provided us with: "A man has nothing better under the sun than to eat, drink and be merry" (8:15). Again the key word of Creation is used: *tov,* "good" (translated here as "better"). The enjoyment Ecclesiastes is speaking about is not " 'Let us eat and drink, for tomorrow we die' " (Isaiah 22:13; 1 Corinthians 15:32). It is a joy of submission, the joy of receiving the gift of God. Not just the joy of eating and drinking, but any joy—the joy of beauty, of rest, of love; the joy of understanding, of hearing God's word, of seeing God's miracles in our life; the joy of being surprised by His answers to our prayers.

On the other side, this joy is accompanied by the pain of our "labor" for the days of our life "under the sun" (8:15). The word for "labor," *'amal,* is the same as the word used in verse 17 to describe the "labor" of "man," or of "the wise" who tries "to know." In verse 16, we read that this "knowing" applies to wisdom, "to see the business that is done on earth." This refers to what is done by humans, all their vain efforts to grasp wisdom and all that is happening in the world (compare 1:13).

In verse 16, our inability to "know wisdom" is suggested through the imagery of sleep, a unique expression in the Bible: "Even though one sees no sleep day or night." How could we "see sleep" while our eyes are closed? Just as we cannot see ourselves sleeping and cannot understand what sleep is, we cannot "see" ourselves being wise. We lack perspective, our eyes are closed. Therefore, we cannot see how wisdom works.

Wisdom is impossible to grasp. In verse 17, this elusiveness of wisdom is repeated three times: "a man cannot find out the work," "yet he will not find it," and "though a wise man attempts to know it, he will not be able to find it." The chapter closes on this failure and frustration about our inability "to know."

Our questions remain suspended in the void. We will never understand. Yet joy, the gift of God, should accompany the anguish of our question. God's answers will help us survive our unanswered questions.

---

1. See Deuteronomy 28:50, where it applies to a cruel and "fierce" nation, which has no respect for the weak; compare Daniel 8:23, where it describes the arrogance of the little horn; compare Proverbs 7:13.

2. See Exodus 22:10, 11; 2 Samuel 21:7; 1 Kings 2:43.

3. Abraham Heschel, *Man's Quest for God: Studies in Prayer and Symbolism* (New York: Scribner, 1954), 150.

4. This phrase means "time of judgment" *(hendiadys),* as attested in many Hebrew manuscripts and the Greek version of the Septuagint.

CHAPTER 10

Surviving Your Questions

The place where Ecclesiastes just left us is not comfortable; our questions about life and destiny are, forever, unanswered. We don't know where we are going, yet we know that we will die. We don't know how to live, what to do, yet we know that we are alive. We don't know how to make sense of nonsense, so we all stumble on it. These are the three basic challenges that Ecclesiastes will submit to us in this chapter.

In His Hand

Chapter 9 begins with the basic principle, the fundamental truth, that will encompass "all" the problems: "I considered all" (Ecclesiastes 9:1). The word "all" *(kol),* key word of the Creation story (see chapter 1), is also a key word in this chapter, occurring fourteen times. In the first verse we hear it three times. Ecclesiastes' perspective is definitely universal. Not only are "all" the problems on the table, but also "all" human categories are considered: the righteous and the wicked, the clean and the unclean, the religious person and the secular person, the righteous and the sinner, the one who commits himself and the one who refuses commitments (9:2). We all have the same fate: we do not know where we are going. We do not know what is before us (9:1); we do not know in advance about our loves or about our hatreds, our pains, or joys. But we all know one thing: we die.

Again Ecclesiastes makes it clear that death is both real and evil. It is real, because death does not allow any hope. It is total. When we die, nothing is left of us. Ecclesiastes does not believe in the immortality of the soul. But he attacks the first argument used by those who would be tempted by this idea. There is no spiritual entity that would survive our body. Indeed, it is clear for all of us that, at death, our body disintegrates. It is a concrete, visible, and palpable reality that we all experience, in various degrees, from the beginning of our life to its end. Our sicknesses, our wounds, and our aging remind us at each moment of our physical mortality. On the other hand, when it comes to the invisible "spiritual" dimension of our being—thinking, remembering, loving—because we do not see it these "things," some people have concluded that they will remain after our bodies don't.

For Ecclesiastes, "the dead know nothing" (9:5). Ecclesiastes is not just talking about the cognitive ability to know information; we may not know and still exist. The "know nothing" of the dead is set in contrast to the living, who "know that they will die" (9:5). The dead do not even have consciousness, no real existence.

Nor can they communicate with the living: "Nevermore will they have a share / In anything done under the sun" (9:6). Not because they are in heaven and we are on earth, nor because it is difficult for them to have access to us, the living. They cannot relate to us because they, simply, do not exist. They do not love, they do not hate, they do not desire (9:6a). All these "spiritual" faculties "have perished" (9:6); they are completely destroyed.

The Hebrew word 'abad, "perish," does not leave any ambiguity. The verb is applied to the political and military destruction of nations (Exodus 10:7; Deuteronomy 8:20; Jeremiah 49:38) and also to the plant in the book of Jonah, which "perished in a night" (Jonah 4:10). 'Abad is also found in parallel with sheol, the place of the dead (Proverbs 15:11; 27:20), and with the grave (Psalm 88:11). The word is used to qualify the end of hope (Ezekiel 19:5; Psalm 9:19; Job 11:20). The verb 'abad ("perish") means total destruction—with no hope whatsoever.

Death is evil because it is real. It is not a passage to a superior state, an inconvenient moment in disguise that ultimately brings a better life. Because there is no such a thing as a soul surviving the body, death contains nothing positive; it is completely negative, and absolutely sad. Ecclesiastes leaves no doubt about it: "They have no more reward" (9:5). There is no paradise or hell after death. It isn't only the death of the young, death by accident or by violent crime, that is bad and out of place. Even the old man Ecclesiastes, after his long and full life, finds death unacceptable.

The Bible, from its first pages, shows that death was not part of the original design. Death came as a result of a human move out of the divine influence (Genesis 2:16, 17). In the context of the Bible, death is seen in connection to evil and sin. As the apostle Paul puts it: "Just as through one man sin entered the world, and death through sin, and thus death spread to all men, because all sinned" (Romans 5:12). In the same manner, Ecclesiastes calls death "an evil" (9:3a) that he relates to the life lived by the sons of men (9:3b).

Ecclesiastes has already specified that this fate will concern the wicked as well as the righteous (9:2). Death will have the same effect on "all" of us. This is why "a living dog is better than a dead lion" (9:4). Through this imagery, Ecclesiastes is not just emphasizing the advantage of life over death but is saying that the live dog, even though sinful and wicked,[1] is better off than the dead lion, no matter how righteous and wise[2] it is. Death is hopeless for all.

Yet within that hopeless condition, Ecclesiastes affirms that "there is hope" (9:4). Nowhere else in the book is this note so clearly sounded. This hope concerns the righteous, who are set in contrast to the wicked: "The hearts of the sons of men are full of evil; madness is in their hearts while they live, and after that they go to the dead" (9:3). "But for him who is joined to all the living," Ecclesiastes remarks, "there is hope" (9:4). The language is reminiscent of Deuteronomy 30:19, the only other text that shares with this verse of Ecclesiastes the particular association of the words *bachar*, "to choose,"[3] and *hayyim*, "life" or "living."[4] A literal translation of the Hebrew text would be "who is the one who chooses."[5] This would mean, then, that our text is alluding to the righteous who "chooses" "to love the LORD . . . to walk in His ways, and to keep His commandments" (Deuteronomy 30:16). We also note that the righteous is in the singular, always a minority; the wicked, in contrast, are in the plural, always a majority (compare Ecclesiastes 7:5).

For Ecclesiastes "there is hope" only for the one who chooses life, who—by choosing righteousness—chooses to be among the living. In fact, the Hebrew word *bitachon,* "hope," means more than "hope." It is not just "something to look forward to,"[6] a pious wish. The word refers to the certainty, the absolute confidence that something surely will happen; it has the connotation of firmness or solidity and expresses the idea of assurance and security. The Psalms contain most of the biblical occurrences of the word (50 out of 181), applying it consistently to express trust in God (Psalm 22:4; 16:9, and other places), especially in a desperate situation, when there is no reason for hope.

In one of the biblical stories, the word is used with particular intensity, namely, when the Assyrian king Rabshakeh challenges Hezekiah's trust in God (2 Kings 18; 19; compare Isaiah 36; 37; 2 Chronicles 32).[7] We know that the king of Assyria had sent "a great army against Jerusalem" (2 Kings 18:17). It was hopeless. Only God's supernatural and miraculous intervention saved the king of Israel from a sure and unavoidable disaster (2 Kings 19:1–7; 35–37).

This is the kind of hope Ecclesiastes is referring to: unbelievable hope, which hangs on nothing. This kind of hope trusts God in the face of death, when you know that there is nothing left for you here, not even a piece of your soul, nothing.

Of course, only the God of creation could meet that challenge because He is the only one who can create out of nothing. Only the miracle of creation could make that operation possible. Ecclesiastes has creation in mind when he says, "The righteous and the wise and their works are in the hand of God" (9:1). The expression "in the hand of God" is typical in the Bible of the language of creation:

Which of all these does not know
    that the hand of the LORD has done this?
In his hand is the life of every creature
    and the breath of mankind (Job 12:9, 10, NIV; compare
34:14, 15; Psalm 104:28–30).

It is with this hope in life out of death that Ecclesiastes moves to the present existence.

Go, Live, and Do!

Hope does not make dreamers. It is highly significant that just after having laid down the nature of hope as a window out of hopeless death, Ecclesiastes turns to the present life and calls for action. Ecclesiastes does not urge us to pray or to meditate; he does not go off in hallelujahs or a beatific expectation; the tone of his voice changes. From the lamenting and reflexive discourse, he shifts to an imperative and pressing mode (9:7–10).

The first imperative, "Go" (9:7), contains and introduces all the others. It is an appeal to move out of the place where we are right now. Abraham heard that verb from God when He called him to leave his country and his father's house (Genesis 12:1). It is an appeal to go to new horizons, knowing that we are in God's hands. Yet, paradoxically, it is not an appeal to sacrifice and to give. Ironically, "God has already accepted your works" (9:7). On the contrary, it is an invitation to receive and to enjoy the gifts of God, the most basic and the most concrete ones, the first gifts of God at the time of Creation. "Eat . . . with joy, / And drink . . . with a merry heart" (9:7). We are so eager to be righteous, to be holy, and to gain God's approval, so eager to give to God in our pious motivations, that our food has lost its flavor and our table is poisoned with bitter disputes and finger pointing.

Let's be clear—Ecclesiastes is not suggesting that we eat and drink anything. We eat from the hands of God, and it is within the gift of God that he calls for enjoyment. So when he urges us to drink wine "with a merry heart," he is not encouraging us to get drunk and be joyful from it. He already expressed himself on this matter and denounced that kind of deception (Ecclesiastes 2:3). The association of "bread and wine" here should not be taken literally; it is, in the Bible, an idiomatic expression to designate the two basic products of the land (as Moses' blessing on Israel attests): "Then Israel shall dwell in safety, . . . In a land of grain and new wine" (Deuteronomy 33:28; compare Genesis 14:18). The technical word *tirosh,* "new wine," which is used in the last passage, is clear enough to indicate that Moses referred to the freshly pressed grape juice.[8] The fact that Ecclesiastes makes the same association of bread and wine as is made elsewhere in the Bible (see Psalm 4:7) suggests that he is also referring to grape juice here.

Ecclesiastes goes even further: He exhorts us to take good care of our appearances: "Let your garments always be white / And let your head lack no oil" (9:8). In the context of the Bible, the reference to "white garments" and "oil" simply means to have always renewed (white) fresh clothes on, and perfume, as an expression of joy and festivity.[9] In other words, put yourself in the mood of celebration, and not in the sad mood of mourning and fasting. This sounds like Jesus, when He warns His disciples, "Do not be like the hypocrites, with a sad countenance. . . . But . . . anoint your head and wash your face" (Matthew 6:16, 17). Religion has often been associated with sadness and deprivation; some think that the more they are sad and the more they do not enjoy life, the closer they are to God. The religion of the Bible stands opposed to that mentality; because God is the Creator, religion implies that we should receive and enjoy what God has given us. The traditional Puritan ideal of strict and rigorous dress and the refusal of physical enjoyment are not the biblical ideal.

Ecclesiastes emphasizes the value and joy of life. He urges us to "live joyfully" (9:9). Interestingly, this phrase applies to conjugal life: "Live joyfully with the wife whom you love all the days of your vain life which He has given you under the sun" (9:9). This is first an invitation to open our eyes to recognize the value and the beauty which is here, as is suggested in the literal translation, "to see life." Life is here, and yet we do not see it. Our eyes may be elsewhere. This means to be attentive to what has been given to us rather than to look other places. It implies gratefulness and faithfulness, the fundamental condition for conjugal happiness. It is doubly imperative—I am grateful because I love her, due to the particular relationship I have with her; and I am grateful because she is God's gift to me, due to the particular relationship I have with God. It is both a movement from me and a movement toward me.

Ecclesiastes expands this idea through the image of the "portion": "For that is your portion in life, and in the labor which you perform under the sun" (9:9). The Hebrew word for "portion," *heleq,* is a technical term for the space allotted to humans in their existence. In the Bible, the term is often associated with "inheritance," referring to the given lot of land in the distribution of the Promised Land

(Joshua 19:9). It is a gift, full of promises, and a responsibility to keep it and use it.

Life in the hand of God is not passive. Ecclesiastes calls us "to do" (9:10). Not the busy work to cover our anguish and give us a quick good conscience, or the mercenary work to please our boss and the society. No—our initiative and our passion are demanded. And yet the work remains within human capacity. We are responsible to find it. We should do it with all the strength at our disposal and yet not overestimate ourselves.

"Whatever your hand finds to do, do it with your might" (9:10). The language of this phrase is reminiscent of creation. The word "all" (*kol*)—here translated by "whatever"—which introduces the phrase, and the repetition of the verb "to do" (*'asah*) are found together in the context of the Sabbath at the conclusion of the Creation story (Genesis 2:1–3). If we add the word *hand,* then we understand that this work by our hand is also a work of creation. The human work is a response to the divine creation. At the same time, it conveys implicitly the truth of the Sabbath commandment, which is the direct human response to creation and which echoes our passage from Ecclesiastes on the same words:

> "Remember the Sabbath to keep it holy. Six days you shall labor and *do all* your work, but the Sabbath day is the Sabbath of the LORD your God. In it you shall *do* no work. . . . For in six days the LORD *made* the heavens and the earth, the sea, and *all* that is in them, and rested the seventh day. Therefore the LORD blessed the Sabbath day and hallowed it" (Exodus 20:8–11, emphasis supplied).

The human imitation of God in work implies the human imitation of God in the Sabbath. Any religious reflection on work should imply a reflection about Sabbath. The reverse is also true: the truth of Sabbath implies a certain philosophy of work. This is why the text about work in Ecclesiastes implies the text of the Sabbath.

The lessons of that connection in the context of this passage of Ecclesiastes are multiple. First of all, work is a human expression of the divine image. We create just as He created. From that perspective, work belongs to the sacred domain. Interestingly, the Hebrew word for *work, 'avodah,* means also "worship." Work is then to be performed with the same sense of sacredness as the worship service. You should work thoroughly, carefully, and attentively, striving to do the best you can.

At the same time, work should stay within human proportions. It is only in proportion to "your might." Work should never crush you; it is in "your hand." You should control it. In that connection, the Sabbath helps place work in its right perspective. This is the day when we are free from work. This is the day when we are all equal, and no one is working for us anymore. This is also the day when we remember the God of Creation: the day of rest when we learn to put ourselves in His hand, trusting Him beyond the grave. Ecclesiastes even refers to the grave in the context of work: "For there is no work or device or knowledge or wisdom in the grave where you are going" (9:10).

Confronting Nonsense

Next, it is only in God's hand that we are able to follow Ecclesiastes' eyes and see what he sees and thus face the unbearable nonsense. Ecclesiastes unwraps his first observation in a poetic fashion. In two stanzas of five verses each, he draws a parallel between the unfairness in life (9:11) and the unfairness of death (9:12).

In the first stanza we are confronted with the unfairness of life: good things happen to bad people, and bad things to good people. One who is not swift wins the race, implying that the swift do not win; the battle is not to the strong, implying that the strong lose it; bread is not given to the wise, implying that it is given to the fool; riches are not for men of understanding, implying that they are for the simpleton; and favor is not to men of skill, implying that skillful men do not benefit from any favor.

On both sides we are surprised by the unexpected. But if on the side of the wise this fate is unfair, on the side of the fool it is a happy ending. Ecclesiastes is not mentioning the failure of the wise. He is merely observing the undeserved success of the fool.

In the second stanza, he draws a parallel between this "unexpected" success and the "unexpected" death that will fall on the sons of men "like fish taken in a cruel net" or "birds caught in a snare" (9:12). The second observation provides us with the key to understanding and accepting the unfairness of the first scenario. Just as death falls unexpectedly on the sons of men, success falls unexpectedly on the fool. The absurd character of death explains the absurd character of success. The reason for success, explains Ecclesiastes, is not merit, it is not God; it is just an accident, with no reason whatsoever: "time and chance happen to them all" (9:11). This statement occupies the center of the poem. And since Ecclesiastes identifies this unexpectedness of death as "evil," the identification also applies to the unexpectedness of success. This kind of success is evil, just as death is.

Ironically, this parallelism places the fool in an uncomfortable position. Likewise, the undeserved success of the fool is related to the trap that caught the bird; success is expected to become a trap for him.

This parallelism also comforts the swift, the strong, the wise, the man of understanding, and the man of skill—all those who deserved to win. Ecclesiastes recognizes the unfairness of their fate. While making this observation, he is at the same time recognizing that they remain on the right side nevertheless. He acknowledges their skill and their wisdom. Success, bread, and riches do not prove anything about the real value of that person. According to Ecclesiastes' scenario, it is in fact the contrary. By acknowledging this, Ecclesiastes disconnects success, bread, and riches from the value of the person, because these things are not values per se. The only real value is the wise man, whose wisdom does not depend on success. It is not because you are rich that you are wise; conversely, it is not because he is poor that he is not wise.

Ecclesiastes illustrates his point with the parable of the poor wise man, whose wisdom saved the little city from the hands of a powerful king. We note in passing the contrast between "the poor man" in "the little city with few men" and the "great king" who "came against it, besieged it, and built great snares around it" (9:14). Out of this conflict the powerful king emerges ridiculous, and the wisdom of the poor man is all the more amazing. And yet no one acknowledges this wise man. The lesson of the parable is that "wisdom is better than strength" even though "the poor man's wisdom is despised" (9:16). We could extend the lesson to the other failures: the swift remains faster even though he lost the race; and the men of understanding and the skillful remain smarter even though they are poor and not popular. Ecclesiastes concludes that one successful sinner, armed with powerful "weapons of war . . . destroys much good" (9:18). The fact that the sinner is successful does not mean that he is good; success is therefore not a value per se. The important thing is not so much what you have achieved and were recognized for; the important thing is who you really are.

---

1. The dog was the most despised animal in Middle Eastern culture, as it haunted the refuse dumps of the towns. In the Bible it was associated with uncleanness, eating of unclean meat (Exodus 22:31), and even of human flesh (1 Kings 14:11). *Dog* was often a term to designate the despised person (1 Samuel 17:43), Israel's enemies, or God's enemies (Psalms 22:16; 59:6), the wicked (Psalm 22:16; Isaiah 56:10, 11). The book of Revelation calls "dogs" those who are excluded from the kingdom of God (Revelation 22:15).

2. The lion was revered for its noble and grand qualities, its power (Proverbs 30:30), and its courage (Proverbs 28:1); it was used as a metaphor to designate Judah (Genesis 49:9), the king (Proverbs 19:12), and God Himself (Job 10:16). In the book of Revelation the Messiah is termed "the Lion of the tribe of Judah" (Revelation 5:5).

3. The traditional Hebrew text (*Masoretic* text) uses *bachar*, "to choose," but a number of versions have preferred to read *chabar*, "to join," on the basis of other manuscripts (see NKJV among others).

4. The Hebrew word *hayyim* means both "life" and "the living ones" (plural of the word *hay*, "living").

5. See C. L. Seow, *Ecclesiastes*, 300.

6. Translation by the *New Jewish Publication Society* (*NJPS*).

7. The word *bitachon* occurs twenty times in these passages.

8. The Hebrew word *tirosh* is derived from the root *yarash*, "to drive out" (compare Micah 6:15). The word *yayin* used by Ecclesiastes (9:7) is ambiguous and could refer both to alcoholic wine and freshly pressed grape juice.

9. Esther 8:15; 2 Samuel 14:2; Psalm 23:5.

CHAPTER 11

The Flies in
the Perfume

The book of Ecclesiastes is full of animals and insects that convey spiritual lessons. As we have already noticed in the story of "the bragging butterfly" (Chapter 1), Solomon was an expert on animals who "spoke also of animals, of birds, of creeping things, and of fish" (1 Kings 4:33). In the preceding chapter he referred to birds and fish (Ecclesiastes 9:12); he also spoke about dogs, lions (9:4), cattle (2:7), and beasts in general (3:19, 21). In this chapter he uses two serpents, a bird, and (of all things!) flies in order to convey his lesson.

Folly spoils wisdom, just as "dead flies putrefy the perfumer's ointment" (10:1). It is always the same problem that bothers Ecclesiastes: the mixture of folly and wisdom. So far, he struggled in trying to identify wisdom apart from folly, to sort out the one from the other, and so he played the accountant (7:27, 29).

Now the situation is getting more dramatic. Folly is not just mingling with wisdom; it penetrates into the cells of wisdom and affects its very identity. Fools are like flies, or to speak a more modern language, like microbes; they are everywhere and have contaminated everything.

In the Schools

This is the last place where fools are expected to be. Yet Ecclesiastes sees them parading in the academic world. Fools are teaching classes from high school to the university. Ecclesiastes sees fools among the professionals of wisdom who specialize in the subject of wisdom. Even the true wise man, originally "respected for wisdom" (10:1), has been corrupted. It is amazing that just "a little folly" does the job. Just a little compromise with error, only one fallacious presupposition, is enough to ruin the whole product. The trouble is that the teaching is garbed in wisdom. Folly has taken over its language, its way of reasoning, and thus becomes all the more respectable.

Think, for instance, of how evolution has been introduced in academic circles and has so invaded all disciplines, all under the noble titles of Science and Reason, that any one who attempts another discourse is suspected of being a "fool." This is exactly the kind of attitude under Ecclesiastes' satiric observation. Suddenly, when it comes to this kind of topic, the wise, who is normally so rational and so concerned with integrity, becomes irrational and may even lose his temper in the discussion.

Ecclesiastes uses the imagery of his time to illustrate this strange behavior: "A wise man's heart is at his right hand, but a fool's heart at his left" (10:2). Ecclesiastes is not giving here a dubious lesson of anatomy. He is just using humor to suggest this man's inconsistency. He does indeed possess wisdom; the heart, the seat of thinking and of wisdom, is there (1:16; 1 Chronicles 29:18; Exodus 31:60). Yet the heart, which gives him the capacity to think with wisdom, is relegated to the left side. This is the side that is usually associated with deception (Judges 3:15, 21; 2 Samuel 20:9, 10), while the right side is the side of blessing and unique capacity (Genesis 48:14; Ezekiel 21:22). Saying that he has his heart "at his left hand" implies that he does not think any more. He is guided only by his guts and prejudices, although this does not keep him from teaching with authority and from saying to others that they are fools (10:3).[1]

Ecclesiastes tells us that the supposed wise man even has the support and the honor of the authorities: "Folly is set in great dignity" (10:6). Again we stumble on the same nonsense he already displayed in the preceding chapter about "the race is not to the swift," and so on (9:11). We hesitate when we encounter the same injustice, which Ecclesiastes denounces as "an error," committed by the ruler: "servants on horses, while princes walk on the ground like servants"

(10:7). The fool is taken seriously and honored, while the wise is humiliated. It is then no wonder that the authority [2] who promoted the fool will lose his temper against you (10:4a). In that case, counsels Ecclesiastes, "Do not leave your post" (10:4b). Remain faithful to your conviction, without losing your temper.[3] "For you may then be able to heal[4] great iniquities"[5] (10:4c).

The Hebrew verb *rp',* translated as "heal," may have to do with reconciliation and forgiveness (see Psalm 60:4; 103:3). The idea is that in remaining calm, with a spirit of peace and forgiveness (while staying firm on your conviction), you may be able to gain the person and thus repair the iniquity caused by folly. James gives the same advice with the same language: "Let him know that he who turns a sinner from the error of his way will save a soul from death and cover a multitude of sins" (James 5:20). It is not enough to be right before the opponent. You also need to create a friendly relationship with him, in such a way that he may be able to listen to you and be convinced.

In the Workplace

Now that the fools are behind their desks and occupy the workplace, we see them in action, and we hear them speaking. They reveal themselves. They are trapped by their work and their words. He has alluded to that prospect, by relating the nonsense of "the race not to the swift" to the nonsense of the "snare" of death (9:11, 12). When we are put in a position, not because of our skills or the right knowledge, but simply because of our good connections and our charming smiles, then the position becomes a trap for us, and in it our foolishness will be exposed.

The first illustration is in fact taken from the domain of traps: "He who digs a pit will fall into it" (10:8). The pit Ecclesiastes is talking about is a trap for animals (see Psalm 7:15; Jeremiah 18:22). Because these traps were camouflaged, the hunters had to be particularly careful; otherwise they would fall into the pit they themselves had dug. The same foolish behavior is noted about the bad mason who is bitten by a serpent hidden between the stones of a wall because he did not know about the nature of those stones; or the bad quarryman who is hurt by the stones he manipulates because he is clumsy; or the bad carpenter who keeps smashing his fingers with the hammer; or the bad woodcutter who does not know how to use his ax and wastes enormous energies for a couple of sticks. Such behavior is ridiculous and inefficient.

What is missing here is the right wisdom. The lesson implied in these proverbs is the same as the first lesson. If the fool has been put in your place of expertise, do not worry! Just wait: the work he will do will be his own trap, and then genuine wisdom, yours, will be needed.

The same observation is made about the words of the fools. The fools were promoted as if they were wise. But when they speak, their tongue reveals who they really are. The first illustration is the snake charmer (10:11). Ecclesiastes uses a very uncommon expression, meaning in Hebrew "the master of the tongue," probably intentionally to refer to the poisonous tongue of the snake and/or to his own tongue that would master the snake. If the snake charmer does not know the right magic words, the right whistling, the right move, or how to read his snake, the snake will bite him; and then he will be revealed as a con man: "the babbler is not different" (10:11). In other words, he is not "better" (literal translation) than any vulgar amateur: He is not "master of the tongue."

This first example anticipates the following verses that speak about the tongue of the fool, which will reveal him as a fool. The face of the speaking fool is rendered in evocative language, almost like a satiric cartoon. "The lips" (10:12) are given in a plural form that is not regularly used for two, implying more than two lips. The fool is so talkative (10:14) that he gives the impression that he has many lips on his mouth. These numerous lips "swallow him up" (10:12). He is devoured by his own words, a self-cannibalism that already characterized the fool in 4:5. From the beginning to the end of his speech (10:13), he is always talking foolishness, so much so that at the end we are still in the beginning. The fool remains forever in the present and does not engage in the future; he does not contribute in anything: "No man knows what is to be" (10:14).

Ecclesiastes concludes his satire about the talkative fool on an ironic note. The fool who was walking "along the way" (10:3), showing the way to everyone and calling everyone a fool, does not know himself "how to go to the city" (10:15). The lesson is striking. The fool is now lost and cannot get any help from anyone because, after all, they are all fools to him. The fool will never find the city and will help no one.

On the Throne

In this last section of the chapter there are no more wise men; only the fools are left. We have therefore no point of reference; no one knows that they are fools. Only an immature child is sitting on the throne. There is no one to counsel him. The princes are busy having parties, even though it is only morning. The situation is alarming: "Woe to you, O land, when your king is a child, / And your princes feast in the morning!" (10:16). A leadership crisis is taking place in the middle of the capital of the "land."[6] The previous verse (10:15) ended with a reference to "the city." If verse 16 speaks about the land, it is because what is happening in the city has repercussions on the whole land. This association of "the king" and "the city" points back to the parable of the city saved by a poor wise man (9:13–15). Only this time, there is no wise man left in the neighborhood to save the city, and a "child" is in power.

The Hebrew word for "child," *na'ar,* is the same word used by Solomon when he qualified himself as "a little child *(na'ar);* I do not know how to go out or come in" (1 Kings 3:7). He asked then for wisdom to help him to govern, which would compensate for his being "a child." The use of the same word in Ecclesiastes implies then the lack of wisdom of this king. The word *na'ar* means also "servant"[7] (Genesis 22:3) and, therefore, someone who is not of a royal descent, thus not supposed to be the king, a usurper.

The princes, the leaders of the nation, are indulging in pleasure even in the morning, and are then unable to face their duties during the day. What is missing in that city is wisdom, legitimacy, and self-control. The consequences of this leadership crisis are disastrous: "The house leaks" (10:18). The word *house* does not just refer to a literal house. The definite article suggests that Ecclesiastes has in mind a national entity. In Hebrew, this word designates the palace (1 Kings 7:8) or, rather, the temple (1 Kings 6:2, 3, 38). These leaders have lost total sense of their responsibilities and of spiritual priorities. They do not care about the management of the city and about the temple. Not only the political life but also worship and religious life are crumbling. These leaders are preoccupied with nothing but partying and money.

The verb "answer" ('anah), which is here associated with money, is often used in the Bible with God as the subject, especially in the Psalms (Hosea 2:21; Psalm 3:5; 13:4, etc.). Furthermore, money is placed in a cosmic perspective, it is related to "all" (kol): "money answers everything" (10:19). Money has taken the place of God. It is all that counts: money, money, money. Wisdom has completely disappeared.

It just started with a few flies in the perfume. At first, the odor was corrupted, wisdom mingled with folly. Then wisdom got contaminated; folly penetrated its texture. Now we reach the final stage: folly is reigning, and wisdom has disappeared. There is no more perfume, only flies. It started in the intimacy of "the heart" (10:2). Then it came out in the open, thanks to one single fool walking and teaching "along the way." Little by little, it entered the academic world (10:3); then it infiltrated the administration (10:6) and became a plural, "servants on horses" (10:7). Then it invaded the offices, the factories, the building sites, and the shops (10:8–11). After that, the words were repeated everywhere in the press—on radio, on TV, on the Internet. Finally, it reached the government (10:16) and the religious headquarters (10:18). The last word of that litany is *all* (10:19). Folly is everywhere.

But not really everywhere. Into the folds of the lamentation, seemingly out of place, sneaks a blessing:

> Blessed are you, O land, when your king is the son of nobles,
> And your princes feast at the proper time—
> For strength and not for drunkenness!" (10:17).

This land is set in contrast to the other land. It is a blessing rather than a curse. This verse is a "beatitude" like those found in the Psalms (pronounced upon the man who is righteous, such as in Psalms 41:1; 65:4; and others). Jesus used the same form in His beatitudes as recorded by Matthew (5:3–12).

The king is legitimate and not an immature servant, not a usurper. He is qualified as "the son of nobles;" the Hebrew word *chorim*, translated "nobles," designates the elite in Israelite society who are supposed to provide the rulers of the kingdom (Isaiah 34:12). The princes "feast at the proper time— / For strength and not for drunkenness" (10:17). There is nothing wrong with "feasting" (the Hebrew is, literally, "eating"), as long as it is done at a proper time and for the purpose of "strength," and not for the purpose of orgies. Good leaders are thus characterized by "strength." The Hebrew word *gebura,* "strength," that is given in opposition to drunkenness implies physical vigor but is also connected with God's spirit, wisdom, and understanding. The "wisdom" in the book of Proverbs testifies to this: "I, wisdom. . . . Counsel is mine, and sound wisdom; / I am understanding, I have strength" (Proverbs 8:12, 14; compare Isaiah 11:2). These leaders are not only physically strong and abstinent, they are also wise and belong to the camp of God.

This group of people is radically different from the others. They could identify with the holy ones who remain faithful to God and His commandments. In 10:20, Ecclesiastes is obviously addressing the people of the blessed land, who have the good king and the good princes, and behave wisely (10:17). Because they belong to the minority, and because folly is everywhere, they are to be careful. Someone may be watching them. Even if the king is immature, even if he is a usurper, "do not curse the king" (10:20). Even if the administration is corrupted, "do not curse the rich" (10:20). And it is not enough to control your words in public. You have to be careful even in the privacy of your bedroom, when you are with your wife only. You even have to be careful when you are asleep, for you may talk in your dreams; someone may hear your words and report you. Ecclesiastes refers to "a bird in the air" (10:20), perhaps a messenger pigeon like the ones that were used in ancient Egypt for communication. The next line specifies literally "a possessor of wings," which could be a bird or also an insect, perhaps a butterfly.

The tone of your voice *(qol)* or your word *(dabar)* could betray you. Jesus sounds the same warning: "Whatever you have spoken in the dark will be heard in the light, and what you have spoken in the ear in inner rooms will be proclaimed on the housetops" (Luke 12:3). In the face of the noisy laughing, feasting, and talkative fools, the wise should be silent and not speak. Ecclesiastes even urges them to control their thoughts: "even in your thought." Because if you think negatively or critically of someone, sooner or later you will betray yourself, if not through your words or the tone of your voice, then through your facial expression or body language. It is not enough to be diplomatic, kind, and sweet in the presence of the bad king or the fool. Our thoughts and our intentions should be in harmony with our attitude.

Like Jesus, Ecclesiastes warns us against hypocrisy. It is not just a matter of prudence. It is also, and perhaps more importantly, an ethical matter. It is not enough to be right and to belong to the holy remnant, to God's people. Ecclesiastes suggests that we should refrain not only from criticizing loudly and finger pointing but also from thinking negatively about the bad king and his princes. Anti-Semitism or anti-Islam, or anti-whatsoever are not in tune with the claim of being "wise." Belonging to the camp of wisdom does not allow you to be angry with the fool (7:9). Even if you "have the truth," and your king is the legitimate king and the others act foolishly, you should still keep silence and not even think that they are fools. Calling someone else a fool is a characteristic of the fool (10:3).

---

1. This interpretation may be implied in the literal translation of the phrase: "He says to all: 'fool he' "; compare *New English Bible:* "calls everyone else a fool."

2. The Hebrew word for *ruler* is *shalit,* which designates an administrator of some sort (Genesis 42:6), but not the ruler or the governor or the king.

3. There is a play on words between the ruler "losing" his temper, and the wise not "leaving" his position; the same word *hanah* is used in both cases, suggesting a connection between the two behaviors.

4. The Hebrew verb *rp'* ("to heal") is used (see note in NKJV).

5. This is our literal translation; note that we have translated the Hebrew word *chata'im* by its primary meaning, "iniquities."

6. The ancient Greek and Syriac versions have it translated "city."

7. A number of English translations render the word as "servant" (NIV; NAB; NRSV) or "slave" (NEB; REB).

CHAPTER 12

The Risks of Holiness

The last word of wisdom was a call for prudence and a recommendation: When foolishness is everywhere and the king is evil, it's no use to fight back, to attempt a revolution, or even to complain, criticize, and "curse the king." It is unproductive, foolish, and sinful. At the end of his long life of struggles against injustice and bigotry, French philosopher Voltaire got so disappointed that he decided to leave public life and "cultivate his garden."

Yet Ecclesiastes is not suggesting that, in the face of iniquity, we flee from action and enjoy a selfish happiness in the little corner of our garden. On the contrary, the best answer to sin is to step out, help others, and enjoy life as much as possible. According to Ecclesiastes, the only response to the evil kingdom is to focus on holiness, to be generous and bold, and to run risks.

The Risk of Giving

After saying, "Do not curse the king," Ecclesiastes now encourages, "cast your bread upon the waters" (Ecclesiastes 11:1). He has moved from the world of words against people, to the world of action on behalf of people; and, then, from restraint and vigilance to openness and risk. For sure, Ecclesiastes' advice sounds strange and even at odds with Middle Eastern culture, where bread is so precious and sacred that one would never dare to cast it away. In fact, if a piece of bread fell on the ground, one would reverently pick it up, kiss it, and put it back on the shelf.

And why "upon the waters"? Is it to feed the fish? The idea is rather that the bread is given to the flow of the river, with the hope that it will come back, "for you will find it after many days."

For Ecclesiastes, water is associated with the idea of coming back (1:7). There is a custom among Sephardic Jews: When someone would go for a trip, the mother would pour some water on the threshold and have him/her walk on it as a good sign that he/she would come back safely. The same thinking is borne out in an old Egyptian proverb: "Do a good deed and throw it in the water; when it dries you will find it."[1]

The point of Ecclesiastes, then, is twofold. On one hand it is an encouragement to run a risk. Water means adventure; we do not know where the bread will go. But water also means risk of disappearance. In biblical thinking, water is associated with nothingness and chaos (Genesis 1:2; Ezekiel 26:19–21). When Micah speaks about God, who "will cast all our sins / Into the depths of the sea" (Micah 7:19), he means that God will forgive our iniquities (Micah 7:18). On the other hand, it is a promise that the good deed will not be lost, since the water will bring it back to you.

Ecclesiastes' language contains a clear religious allusion. The expression "upon the waters" is associated in biblical tradition with the event of creation (Genesis 1:2). In using this specific expression, Ecclesiastes is suggesting that God, the Creator, is in control. The injunction to "cast the bread upon the waters" is then more than a mere invitation to charity; it is an appeal to faith. You will have your bread come back to you only if you run the risk of losing it. And faith implies this risk. This paradox is in tune with Ecclesiastes' constant reminder that wisdom may be found in the heart of folly and vice versa. This folly of casting your bread is a wise move, because in letting go of it you will find it. Jesus plays with the same paradox when he says, "He who finds his life will lose it, and he who loses his life . . . will find it" (Matthew 10:39).

The truth hidden in Ecclesiastes' proverb has many applications. Of course it first relates to giving the bread to the poor (and not to the rich). By giving bread to the poor, you run the risk that you will not receive anything in return. You do this gesture because the importance of the gift is not you, but the person you give to. If you give with the expectation of rewards, whether it is simply the gratefulness of the poor, some kind of service in return, or even the reward of a good conscience, it is not a gift but self-gratification.

The same applies to spiritual matters. If we serve God in order to be blessed or in order to feel good, or even in order to earn the kingdom of God, we are not serving God, but ourselves. Religion has too often been understood as a give-in-order-to-receive arrangement between humans and God, like some kind of a bank investment. We give our offerings, we go to religious meetings and make our sacrifices for God, and then we expect in return, we even demand, that He will protect us and send us in abundance what we have given. If this happens, if we end up being rich and happy, then we think that we deserved it; if not, we wonder about this God, and sooner or later we will stop giving and even turn away from this God.

It is not the first time that Ecclesiastes addresses this misconception. Earlier, he was observing that this reasoning did not match the reality of life: "The race is not to the swift . . . Nor bread to the wise" (9:11). Now, he provokes the unfairness of the situation, urging us to give without expectation. But he does not say that giving will end up with nothing. He is simply emphasizing that the giver should expect nothing. It is interesting that the bread is "found," which means that it comes as a surprise. In Ecclesiastes' thinking, "finding" is always associated with failure. The only sure thing that Ecclesiastes finds is that he cannot find (7:27, 28; 8:17). The bread is found only "after many days," that is, when we already have forgotten about it. Even with the faith that God is behind it all, when the miracle takes place and we find the bread, we are surprised. We did not expect it. We did not deserve it. It is pure grace, and therefore our hearts are full of gratitude toward God.

Ecclesiastes is not just speaking about a single act of charity. "Give a serving to seven, and also to eight" (11:2). The Hebrew for "serving" is *heleq,* which means "portion." Divide your bread into seven or even eight portions. Share your bread with seven or eight people. The numbers should not be taken literally (see Micah 5:5). This is a literary device to suggest a great number, and even more. The intention is again to encourage liberality. But this time, Ecclesiastes expands the request. The invitation to give freely is extended not just to one person, but to many.

The Risk of Faith

Two arguments are given to convince the giver to be generous. The first argument is negative, addressing the fear of disasters (11:2–4). The second argument is positive and refers to "the works of God" (11:5). Both arguments are based on the risk of faith. The phrase "we do not know" is repeated four times (11:2, 5, 6) and is related to both arguments. "We do not know," therefore we should not fear to give. "We do not know," therefore we should trust.

The fear of troubles is illustrated by the natural elements: the clouds and the rain upon the earth, the tree falling to the south or to the north, the wind, and the sowing and reaping farmer in the fields. These are phenomena that humans cannot comprehend or control: "Indeed, can anyone understand the spreading of the clouds, / The thunder from His canopy?" (Job 36:29). The falling of the tree and the blowing of the wind are both unpredictable. Just as "we do not know" where the tree will fall, to the north or to the south, that is, anywhere,[2] we do not know where the wind will blow. In the book of Ecclesiastes, the wind is a symbol of what's unpredictable and unreliable. This idea is repeated in the book through the recurring expression "grasping for the wind" (1:14; 2:11, 17, 26; 4:4, 6, 16; 6:9), which means impossible to grasp (see also 1:6).

Yet, argues Ecclesiastes, the unpredictability of these elements does not keep the farmer from sowing and reaping. If the farmer had to depend on the elements to sow and to reap, he would do neither. Risk, therefore, is a necessary factor for survival: "He who observes the wind will not sow, / And he who regards the clouds will not reap" (11:4). If you do not want to give because you are afraid of the wind, then you will not sow or reap because of that fear. This fear is ridiculous and even dangerous, because it may bring starvation and death. The fear to give, as a measure of prudence because you are afraid to lose, will ultimately lead you to lose everything.

The work of God is illustrated by "the way of the wind," and the formation of the child in the womb of the pregnant woman. Just as "you do not know" where the wind goes and where it comes from, and "you do not know" how the bones grow in the womb of the mother, "so you do not know the works of God who makes all things" (11:5). Creation is the key to those mysteries, as it is to the mysteries of the natural elements. Significantly, "the way of the wind" points to the wind that was behind the clouds, the fall of the tree, and the act of sowing and reaping. Likewise, the "fullness" of the pregnant woman, which anticipates the child, points to the "fullness" of the clouds, which anticipates the rain. All these phenomena, whether perceived as negative or positive, manifest God's power of creation. The wind, or the spirit (in Hebrew, it is the same word, *ruach*) alludes to the *ruach* that "was hovering over the face of the waters" (Genesis 1:2), anticipating the divine act of creation. In the same manner, the imagery of pregnancy, implicit in the "fullness" of the cloud and explicit in the "fullness" of the woman, and the reference to the growing of the bones, allude to the mysterious process of creation. It is interesting that Jesus associated these two images as He described the birth from above to Nicodemus: "The wind blows where it wishes, and you hear the sound of it, but cannot tell where it comes from and where it goes. So is everyone who is born of the Spirit" (John 3:8).

Faith in creation is behind the act of giving the bread, just as it is behind the act of giving ourselves to God. The act of giving, then, becomes the expression of our faith in God's power of creation. Not just because we trust God even in our loss, but simply because we recognize that, as His creatures, we totally depend on Him. Just as God is described in the Creation story as the one who "gives," those who believe in God as their Creator ought to "give"—not in order to receive, but as their natural and obvious response to what they have received from Him. The grace of God who gives compels us to give.

So the immediate lesson from this object lesson is action. Whether we sow in the evening, in the morning, or both in the evening and in the morning, the result does not depend on us. Therefore, concludes Ecclesiastes, run the risk to sow at any time, because "you do not know" (11:6). What we do not know is the "good" of God's conclusion: "you do not know . . . whether both alike will be good" (11:6). The word "good" *(tov)*, the key word of Creation, is the last word of the paragraph. God's grace, even in our gift, has the last word. Paradoxically, the implication of faith in God is not passivity and laziness (because we trust God, shouldn't we just let Him do the job for us?). On the contrary, the lesson is a call for responsibility and diligence, yet in full tension with the idea of God's grace. Even my gift is the gift of God.

The Risk of Life

Our eyes are flooded with the grace of God. Again the key word of Creation, "good" *(tov)*, is used, as if it had bounced like a ball from the last paragraph (11:6). This "good" (translated "pleasant" in the NKJV) applies now to the light of the sun we see with our eyes: "The light is sweet, / And it is pleasant for the eyes to behold the sun" (11:7). In Hebrew language, the idiom "to see the sun" means simply "to be alive" (6:5; 7:11; see also Psalms 49:19; 58:8; Job 3:16). For light was the first manifestation of life. It all started with the flood of light: " 'Let there be light'; and there was light. . . . the first day" (Genesis 1:3, 5). Our text (11:7, 8) is saturated with references to the creation account of Genesis 1. The words "good," "see," "light," "sun," "living," "man" (Adam), "darkness," and "all" are shared between the two texts. Thus, when Ecclesiastes says, right after the reference to light, "remember the days of darkness" (11:8), he has the Creation text in mind; he urges us to remember where we come from, out of nothing, out of darkness. We did not exist, and here we are enjoying sunshine.

Life is the gift of God; therefore, enjoy it fully. This enjoyment is turned to the past and is related to the memory of our genesis and our gratefulness to the Creator. But this first implication is mixed with another one, which points to the future. The "remember," which naturally implies a reference to the past, also contains a reference to the future.

Enjoy it all the more that light is threatened by darkness: "days of darkness, . . . they will be many" (11:8). Here Ecclesiastes is referring to death, days that should come only after many years of life. We should anticipate a lengthy stay in darkness, "many days," just as we may enjoy a long life, "many years."

Ecclesiastes is not advocating a mediocre philosophy of happiness. The enjoyment is comprehensive. Not just one moment, or a few experiences, such as, perhaps, some shopping once in a while to make yourself feel better. No half measures. Ecclesiastes urges us to exploit "all," to squeeze "all" the juice out of the fruit. Laziness, or the incapacity to "see" and take advantage of the opportunity, is foolish. As much as we can, we should be eager to know "all," to visit every place in the world, to taste every fruit, to get acquainted with all kinds of people, and to learn everything. The risk of death takes us to the risk of life.

Then the call to joy is pressed on the youth. This is the moment in life when we can do the most. We have more time. We have more strength. We have more appetite. We dare more. Ecclesiastes uses the reference to youth as the paradigm for his reflection about the risk of life. Ecclesiastes first recognizes our freedom, our capacity to choose. Happiness is constructed to the measure of our freedom. The more we can do things, the happier we are. This is precisely what Ecclesiastes is saying to the youth. Just "walk in the ways of your heart" (11:9). In biblical thinking, the heart, the center of our being, is the seat of our emotions, our intimate thinking, our desires, and our intentions.

Ecclesiastes again refers to the eyes: "And in the sight of your eyes" (11:9). Whatever you see, whatever comes to your mind, go ahead, "walk" into it, take it, and enjoy it. Ecclesiastes is urging youth to do just what he recommended earlier in general terms. He endorses the same risk of life.

He adds, however, "But know that for all these / God will bring you into judgment" (11:9). Previously, he had just called for remembrance. The darkness of death is a natural part of our life; it is something we just need to "remember." Judgment, however, is not. The definite article, *the* judgment, points to a single specific event and not to some kind of general judicial activity. Judgment is therefore something we need to be informed about.

Ecclesiastes uses the verb "to know." In the preceding paragraph, "to remember" was used as an incentive for enjoyment. In this verse, "to know" is also used in connection to the enjoyment of life. Not to discourage us and put fears into our joys, but, on the contrary, to sanctify our joys.

This new information is not a mere theological doctrine to scare the believer. Judgment is given, not *against* the enjoyment of life, but as an addition, in coordination with it.[3] While darkness was a threat to life and was therefore used as an incentive to enjoy life, the judgment of God is brought as a supplement to life, an incentive for shaping life: "Therefore remove sorrow from your heart / And put away evil from your flesh" (11:10). Although the judgment of God is an external event that will take place at some unknown time in the future (see 3:17), it should affect my life and the way I enjoy it. How interesting (and certainly significant) that the first implication of judgment concerns "sorrow." The Hebrew word *ka'as* for "sorrow" covers the ideas of "sadness" (1 Samuel 1:8), "anxiety" (1 Samuel 1:16), and "bitterness" (Hosea 12:14), and is associated with "anger" (Deuteronomy 9:18) and jealousy (Job 5:2). In Ecclesiastes, it is associated with "pain" and "sickness" (1:18; 2:23: 5:17). In summary, the word expresses everything negative that is the opposite of enjoyment.

The first lesson of the judgment is that we should eliminate anything that would keep us from enjoying life and developing our capacity to enjoy. Judgment reminds us that enjoyment is not only allowed or tolerated by God; it is a divine imperative, our divinely assigned "portion." It is the gift of God; He will call us to account for failure to enjoy. A tradition recorded in the Talmud warns us, "Everyone will give an account before God of all good things one saw in life and did not enjoy."[4]

The second implication of judgment is our responsibility to "put away evil from our flesh." This means that enjoyment of life is to be understood and lived apart from evil. Enjoyment of life does not mean abusing our bodies and ignoring the basic rules of health and life; it does not mean lying to or slandering and harming our neighbor. Enjoying life in the light of the judgment of God is the assignment of wisdom, sorting out the good from the bad, and shaping our life in such a way that it will come out even more enjoyable.

The knowledge of judgment gives, then, a special taste to my enjoyment of life. As the apostle Paul puts it: "Therefore, having these promises, beloved, let us cleanse ourselves from all filthiness of the flesh and spirit, perfecting holiness in the fear of God" (2 Corinthians 7:1). The risks of life end here, on the path of holiness.

---

1. *Instruction of Anksheshonq,* 19, 1. 10, in *AEL* III, 174.

2. The reference to the north and to the south, the two opposite poles, is a literary device to suggest totality (merism).

3. The *waw* that precedes the Imperative *da',* "to know" is the conjunction of coordination "and"; there is no reason why it should be translated as a disjunctive *waw* ("but") implying a contrast with the preceding sentences. As a matter of fact, there is *waw* ("and") before all the preceding verbs (except the introductory verb "rejoice"), which suggests a series of operations: "and let your heart . . . and walk in the ways of your heart . . . and in the sight of your eyes . . . and know." Many translators like to render "but" instead of "and" because they take this line as an additional gloss inserted by a later orthodox editor, to qualify the call to enjoy.

4. *Jerusalem Talmud, Qiddushin,* 4:12.

The End of
the World

Ecclesiastes will take us now to new horizons with a second call to remember Creation (Ecclesiastes 12:1). The first call to remember Creation (11:8) preceded the call to "know" the judgment (11:9), while this second call to remember Creation *follows* the call to know the judgment (11:9).

This sequence is not accidental. The first call to Creation was turned to the past. It was a reference back to the past event of Creation; the passing from darkness to light, from chaos to existence. This second call to remember Creation looks ahead to an event that should come chronologically after the judgment, that is, in the future.

In chapter 12 the orientation shifts from an individual to a cosmic perspective. While the call to remember Creation in 11:7 was related only to the personal life, "if a man lives many years," the call to remember Creation in 12:1 is related to cosmic events: "the sun and the light / and the moon and the stars grow dark" (12:2, NIV). While the call to think of judgment in 11:9 was related to individual judgment, "God will bring *you* into judgment," the reference to judgment in 12:14 is cosmic:

God will bring *every work* into judgment,
Including *every secret thing*,
Whether it is good or whether it is evil (emphasis supplied).

Ecclesiastes calls for our personal response to God in connection to these two events: "Remember your Creator"[1] (12:1), "Fear God and keep His commandments" (12:13). And in order to take these two appeals seriously, he inserts between them a parenthesis about the authority and the inspiration of his words (12:9–12).

Remember Your Creator

After an allusion to old age (12:1), Ecclesiastes moves on to something more terrible than old age: "The sun and the light / and the moon and the stars grow dark" (12:2, NIV). The text (12:2–6) is not about old age (as commonly interpreted) but about the time of the end.[2]

Ecclesiastes warns us about the coming of "the difficult days" (12:1), literally, "the days of evil." The expression, as such, is unique in the Bible. Normally, the Bible uses only the indefinite singular "day of evil," as is the case in 7:14, referring to some particular period in life. The expression "the days of evil" means something different from a vague period in life, whether bad times or old age. The definite article clearly suggests that Ecclesiastes has in mind a specific moment in time, a moment that surpasses the individual. The way the events are introduced is typical of the eschatological language: "in that day when" (12:3).

This is the way that the great day of the coming of the Lord is introduced in biblical prophecies:

The day of the LORD is near. . . .
The sun and the moon will grow dark,
And the stars will diminish their brightness. . . .
in that day . . .
A fountain shall flow from the house of the LORD (Joel 3:14–18; compare Zechariah 3:10).

The luminaries of the sky darken: "the sun and the light / and the moon and the stars grow dark" (12:2, NIV). Therefore, the event of our text is far more cosmic and universal than some personal difficulty such as old age or death. The imagery is, indeed, eschatological and apocalyptic.

This is also the last time the sun is mentioned. Until now, the sun has always been shining. In the beginning, Ecclesiastes had observed the regular course of the sun, rising and setting (1:5), a sign that "there is nothing new under the sun" (1:9). But now the sun is darkened, along with the other sources of light, a sign showing that something new is happening in the history of the world. This is the same sign the prophet Joel understands as announcing the coming of the Lord:

The sun and moon grow dark
And the stars diminish their brightness. . . .
The day of the LORD is great and very terrible. . . .
The sun shall be turned into darkness
And the moon into blood
Before the coming of the great and terrible day of the Lord (Joel 2:10, 11, 31).

Speaking about the great tribulation of the end, Jesus predicts the same cosmic event: " 'In those days, after that tribulation, the sun will be darkened, and the moon will not give its light. . . . Then they will see the Son of Man coming in the clouds with great power and glory' " (Mark 13:24, 26).

The image of the blossoming almond tree (12:5) is also used in the Bible as a sign of God's soon coming. The Hebrew word for almond tree, *shqd*, conveys the idea of "watchfulness" and "alertness." This tree, which in Israel blossoms as early as January or February, is considered as the harbinger of spring. When the prophet Jeremiah receives the vision of a blossoming almond tree *(shqd)*, God interprets the vision playing on the meaning of the word: " 'for I am ready *(shqd)* to perform My word' " (Jeremiah 1:12).

The women[3] who stop working at the mill (12:3), and the fact that "they are few" there, suggests that something terrible has happened suddenly. The image of the abrupt disappearance of workers belongs to the course of events taking place at the time of the end. According to Jesus, " 'Two women will be grinding at the mill: one will be taken and the other left' " (Matthew 24:41). The next verse confirms the silencing of the mill, along with the closing of the gates of the *shuq,* (12:4), that is, the market place (not just "the streets"), a dramatic indication of the end of all economic and social activities.

The atmosphere of desolation and absolute death is dense: We hear the voice of the birds of prey,[4] the mourning of "the daughters of music" sitting on the ground, (12:4) and the wailing of "the mourners" who "go about the streets" (12:5). We see humanity (*'adam*) going to the grave (12:5), and we see and hear the breaking of pitchers (12:6). This latter image reflects a funerary custom still observed among some Jews, the breaking of the menorah lamp, probably in the form of a tree of life, represented by the silver cord (the wick) with the golden bowl.[5]

This vision of terror reaches its climax with the absolute end: the return of the *ruach,* the breath of life (translated as "spirit" in the NKJV), to "God who gave it" (12:7). Like the sun, this is the last appearance of the *ruach* in Ecclesiastes. The first mention of *ruach* was about the restless wind blowing back and forth; in the book, the *ruach* was never caught; it was always unpredictable. Now, the *ruach* returns to God, its source. The world and humanity have come to an end.

Yet Ecclesiastes places this whole dreadful description of the time of trouble under the perspective of Creation: "Remember your Creator" (12:1, 6). The charge is given twice, in the beginning and at the end of the vision. Of course, it is an appeal to examine our lives in the light of this prospect; but it is also a word of assurance, to remind us that beyond darkness, there is light (see 11:8). The Creator is still in control. This is actually the last idea of the poem: "God who gave it" (12:7). The *ruach,* life, is in God's hand. We end, then, with a perspective of hope, trusting the Creator that He will give again. It is significant that the sevenfold vanity, which was identified in the beginning of the book as the stage of darkness preceding creation, is repeated here: " 'Vanity of vanities,' says the Preacher, 'all is vanity' " (12:8). This correspondence suggests that here also creation should follow, that it *will* follow.

Words of Truth

At this juncture, Ecclesiastes opens a parenthesis (12:9–11), looks back at his work, including this book, and echoes his autobiographical introduction (1:1). Again, the third person is used,[6] as was the case in the beginning (1:1, 12). Also, Ecclesiastes refers again to his ruling function—"he still taught the people" (compare "king in Jerusalem" 1:1)—and to the "words" of wisdom.

After that, Ecclesiastes gives a short lecture about the discipline of "wisdom." The prerequisite for wisdom is "to listen"[7] (12:9, author's translation). If we are not open and attentive to the words, they will not reach us. We remember this was Solomon's request to God: " 'give me a listening heart' " (1 Kings 3:9, author's translation). Listening is the basis for the rest to come. Once you have heard and received and paid careful attention to the words, you may then dig into them to understand them thoroughly, and only then you may give them new meanings. This was Ecclesiastes' method. Guided by the Holy Spirit, he compiled pieces of wisdom from his own Israelite tradition; from the poet David, his father; and from ancient Near Eastern literature.

He did not content himself to receive and borrow from the others: He "set in order" (12:9) this material. The Hebrew verb *tiqen,* which has been translated "to make straight" (7:13), implies the ideas of renovation, repair, and improvement. Ecclesiastes was not just a studious scribe; he was also creative. He was an ingenious artist and an original thinker. Ecclesiastes adds that "words of truth" should also be "delightful" (12:10, NAS). Truth should be delivered with artistry. The book begins and ends with a beautiful poem and contains many stylized proverbs, harmonious parallelisms, plays on words, and humorous puns. The rigor and depth of truth does not exclude beauty. Ecclesiastes worked hard and skillfully to produce his masterpiece.

Yet this text is not merely the product of his labor. Throughout the book, Ecclesiastes insisted that human wisdom is just vanity and worthless; only divine wisdom is to be sought. Ecclesiastes qualifies these words as "upright—words of truth" (12:10). The Hebrew word translated as "upright," *yashar,* is the word Ecclesiastes uses to characterize God's work (7:29). The expression "words of truth" *(divrey 'emet)* is associated with God (2 Samuel 7:28; Psalm 119:43; compare Daniel 8:12).

For Ecclesiastes, then, these words are inspired by God. And at the end of his speech, he emphasizes again that "the words of the wise are . . . [he has just referred to himself as 'wise' in 12:9] given by one Shepherd" (12:11). Within the Bible, the metaphor of the shepherd to represent God is very familiar (Psalm 23:1; Ezekiel 34; John 10). The qualification "one" *('ahad)* points to God (Deuteronomy 6:4). But the most striking evidence that this shepherd is God is that the word "shepherd" is the subject of the verb "to give," which accompanies this phrase. As we already pointed out several times, this verb is a key word in the Creation story, and in Ecclesiastes it is always associated with God. In the book of Daniel we find the same idea: God is the one who "gives" wisdom (Daniel 1:17). The verb "to give" betrays then the identity of the subject: It is God.[8] All these "words of the wise" are "given" by God.

Ecclesiastes has just given us a lesson about the tension that characterizes the complex process of inspiration. This text is the result of both the human endeavor and the hand of God. Although it is written in human language, within its specific culture, it remains essentially the gift of God. This relates to the mystery of incarnation and is therefore beyond our human comprehension; as Ecclesiastes would say, "Though a wise man attempts to know it, he will not be able to find it" (8:17).

No wonder Ecclesiastes notes at the end of his inspired words: "Be warned, my son, of anything in addition to them" (12:12, NIV). This formula is loaded with the acute awareness of the sacredness and divine inspiration of these words. It is a strong affirmation of the completeness and sufficiency of the text. The book of Revelation ends the same way: "I warn everyone who hears the words of the prophecy of this book: If anyone adds anything to them, God will add to him the plagues described in this book. And if anyone takes words away from this book of prophecy, God will take away from him his share in the tree of life" (Revelation 22:18, 19, NIV). The book of Ecclesiastes presents itself then as totally inspired and warns us against any attempt to be eclectic about it.

The intriguing image of the "well driven nails" by the shepherd confirms this idea. The "words of the wise," like those "well driven nails," are intended to induce better behavior, as do the spikes at the end of sticks to be used as prods for the sheep; but they are also "well driven," which means that they are so firmly implanted that they are immovable. Maybe the two ideas are related. The words of wisdom, as driven by the Great Shepherd, should disturb us and make us feel uncomfortable; because they do so, we are tempted to remove the nails. It is possible that in the book of Ecclesiastes there are some disturbing nails; and, therefore, we would like to remove them. This metaphor and the warning that follows should prevent us from doing just that.

Ecclesiastes continues in the same mood, not without some irony, saying that beyond those words of wisdom there is no need to add more writing or searching: "Of making many books there is no end, and much study[9] is wearisome to the flesh" (12:12). This verse is not a polemic against writing books and studying (see 1:13). Again, it is a warning against the vanity of human wisdom. Neither is the intention of this statement to rule out the inspiration of other books, since we find the same kind of closing formula elsewhere in the Bible (Deuteronomy 4:2; 12:32; Revelation 22:18, 19). The last word, then, is an appeal that we should receive the whole document as the complete and sufficient word of God. We should not pay attention only to those parts we understand and feel comfortable with, and dismiss what are difficult and disturbing. If we take "all" his words seriously, we will then "hear" his last word seriously.

Fear God and Keep His Commandments

Then Ecclesiastes comes back to the line of discourse he had left earlier (12:8) and brings it to a conclusion: "Let us hear the conclusion of the whole matter" (literally, "the end of the word: all we shall hear," 12:13). This phrase is not intended only to conclude; it is also designed to embrace "all." Not only the whole message of Ecclesiastes is supposed to be contained in this conclusion; it also concerns all humanity: "this is the whole duty of man," or literally, "this is *all* humanity"(12:13). The word *'adam* is used. The word *all* attached to *man* responds to the *all* attached to the *we shall hear*:

"*All* we shall hear" (12:13a)
"This is *all* humanity" (12:13b)

The hearing of Ecclesiastes' words should lead to the reaction of all humans.

This human reaction is then connected to the judgment: "Fear God and keep His commandments. . . . For God will bring every work into judgment" (12:14). It is not the first time that Ecclesiastes refers to the "fear of God" (3:14; 5:7; 7:18; 8:12). Each time, this qualification characterized the camp of the wise and the righteous, those who stood on the right side. In verse 13, the expression is explained:[10] "keep His commandments."

The fear of God is not an abstract concept or an emotional experience; rather, it is related to the idea of "seeing"[11] and expresses the

125

acute consciousness of God's eye upon us: "The eye of the LORD is on those who fear Him" (Psalm 33:18; Job 28:24–28). It is associated with love and justice, and is a way of life: "And now, Israel, what does the LORD your God require of you, but to fear the LORD your God, to walk in all His ways and to love Him, to serve the LORD your God with all your heart and with all your soul, and to keep the commandments of the LORD. . . . Indeed heaven and the highest heavens belong to the LORD your God, also the earth with all that is in it" (Deuteronomy 10:12–14). The fear of God is the essence of biblical religion. It is not an ethereal sentiment or an abstract doctrine; it is a dynamic relationship. For Ecclesiastes, the fear of God is the direct implication of the judgment: "for God will bring every work into judgment" (12:14).

Throughout the book, Ecclesiastes was longing for that moment. His struggles against evil, his litanies on death, his anguish about the emptiness and the senselessness of life and of the world, his revolts against injustice and oppressions, his unanswered questions, his feelings of hopelessness, his cynicism about this world of vanity—all these articulated his call for repair and his nostalgia for a new order.

Judgment is the response to that longing. The book of Psalms is inhabited with the same longing; a shout is repeated over and over again: "How long?" It is the cry of the oppressed longing for deliverance (Psalms 6:3; 13:2; 62:3; 74:10; 94:3, and others). In the book of Daniel, a heavenly being asks the same question with regard to the unbearable suffering of the innocent (Daniel 8:13). To that question, invariably the same answer is given: the judgment of God. In Jewish liturgy, this longing has found its best place in the heart of Kippur, the Day of Atonement. This is the only day when "all the sins" of "all the congregation of Israel," and even the temple (the world in "microcosm"[12]) were under God's investigation (Leviticus 16). This day anticipated the great day when

> God will bring every work into judgment,
> Including every secret thing,
> Whether it is good or whether it is evil" (Ecclesiastes 12:14).

Ecclesiastes concludes his book on that intense longing: the hope for judgment and Creation, which was associated with the

Day of Atonement,[13] the hope for salvation. This is what judgment means in the context of the Bible. The word *judgment* does not resonate well in our culture because the idea of judgment is associated with punishment and anxiety. On the contrary, in the ancient Israelite society, the judge was perceived as the savior; there were no attorneys then; one went to the judge to be vindicated and delivered from injustice. This is why the Day of Atonement was lived as a day of salvation.

It is interesting and highly significant that the third angel's message of Revelation 14, which is also a message about judgment and Creation and is connected with the Day of Atonement,[14] shares a number of key motifs and associations of thought with the conclusion of Ecclesiastes (12:14): Creation, fear of God, judgment, keeping the commandments of God, and universal scope:

... to those who dwell on the earth—*to every nation, tribe, tongue, and people*— ... *"Fear God* and give glory to Him, for the hour of His *judgment* has come; and worship Him who *made heaven and earth, the sea and springs of water* ... here are those who *keep the commandments of God* and the faith of Jesus" (Revelation 14:6, 7, 12, emphasis supplied).

The text of Revelation 14 indicates that the proclamation of judgment anticipates the coming of the Son of Man and the salvation of the world (Revelation 14:14), suggesting the horizon of this passage of Ecclesiastes. Beyond the last words of Ecclesiastes on judgment, a new world is then expected—a new world of justice and peace, free from evil. For the first time wisdom will not fail, because God will finally have sorted out the good and the evil. The whole book of Ecclesiastes was aiming at this cleansing operation, the ultimate work of divine wisdom.

The beginning of the book had taken us into the context of Sukkot, the Feast of Tabernacles: it was loaded with the message of vanity, telling us that everything in our world and in our life was transitory, bound to destruction. But the end of the book takes us into the context of Kippur, the Feast of Judgment. This conclusion is loaded with the message of hope: the perspective of "a new heaven and a new earth," purified from all evil, where there is no death, and where no one will be able to destroy.

Not even our bragging butterfly.

---

1. As for the plural form of the verb *bara'*, it does not necessarily mean that God is in the plural (implying perhaps the idea of trinity, or "plural of majesty"). It has a simple grammatical reason; the *yod* after the *alef* of *bara'* is not the *yod* of plural, but is due to the frequent confusion in Hebrew of the *alef* with the *hey* in the conjugation of the verb.

2. The eschatological interpretation of this passage has been advocated since the Middle Ages and more recently by authoritative biblical scholars, including Fox and Seow. See Seow, p. 374.

3. The word *grinders* is in the feminine gender in Hebrew.

4. According to the syntax of the Hebrew phrase, the subject of the verb *rise* is unspecific, suggesting that it is the voice of the birds that rises. Besides, the interpretation that the verse refers to the old man who would "rise up at the sound of a bird," does not make sense, since an old man would be either deaf or inclined to sleep, he would not be bothered with quiet sounds like the twittering of birds.

5. See Seow, p. 364.

6. The reference to the third person and the retrospective style of the epilogue do not indicate a different author. The same usage has been attested in ancient Egyptian literature (see *Instruction of Kagemni,* from the Sixth Dynasty [2300–2150 B.C.] in *AEL* I, 58–60; see M. V. Fox, "Frame-Narrative and Composition in the Book of Qohelet," *Hebrew Union College Annual* 48 (1977): 85–106.

7. The Hebrew word is *'izzen,* from the word *ozen,* which means "ear." The NKJV translates "ponder," deriving the word from *mo'znayim,* which means "scales," a usage that is unattested elsewhere in the Bible. Besides, this idea of "weighing" and "evaluating" thoughts, in use in Western cultures, is foreign to the ancient Near East.

8. This is the prevailing view in most commentaries.

9. The Hebrew word *lahag* was translated by NKJV as "study," perhaps under the influence of the Latin translation, the Vulgate (*"meditatio,"* that is, "meditation"). However, it should rather mean "talking"; see the Talmud (b. *Erub.* 21b); compare Proverbs 8:7.

10. The *waw* that precedes "keep" is a *waw* of explanation, meaning, "that is."

11. It is possible that the Hebrew verb *ra'ah* ("to see") is etymologically related to the Hebrew verb *yr'ah* ("to fear"), as attested in ancient Egyptian language.

12. See J. Levenson, *Creation and the Persistence of Evil* (San Francisco: Harper & Row, 1988), 78–99.

13. For the association of judgment and Creation at the Day of Atonement, see J. Doukhan, *Secrets of Daniel* (Hagerstown, Md.: Review and Herald®, 2000), 126–132.

14. On the connection between the Day of Atonement and the three angels' message, see J. Doukhan, *Secrets of Revelation* (Hagerstown, Md.: Review and Herald®, 2001), 133–135.